*Reform and resistance in the
international order*

Reform and resistance in the international order

IAN CLARK

Lecturer in Politics
University of Western Australia

CAMBRIDGE UNIVERSITY PRESS

Cambridge
London   New York   New Rochelle
Melbourne   Sydney

Published by the Press Syndicate of the University of Cambridge
The Pitt Building, Trumpington Street, Cambridge CB2 1RP
32 East 57th Street, New York, NY 10022, USA
296 Beaconsfield Parade, Middle Park, Melbourne 3206, Australia

First published 1980

Photoset and printed in Malta by Interprint Limited

Library of Congress cataloging in publication data
Clark, Ian, 1949–

Reform and resistance in the
international order.

Includes bibliographical references
and index.

1. World politics – 19th century.
2. World politics – 20th century.
3. International relations. I. Title.
D363.C68   327'.09   79-54017

ISBN 0 521 22998 7 hardcovers
ISBN 0 521 29763 X paperback

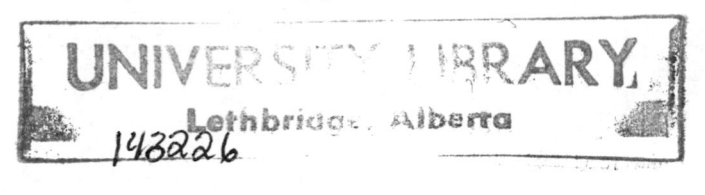

Contents

Introduction:
the 'whig' and 'tory' interpretations

The purpose of this book is to explore the nature of international order and its potential for reform. It seeks to shed some light on the questions raised by Meinecke: 'is this no more than a continual movement to and fro? Or do any organic developments take place here? How far is statecraft timeless, in general, and how far is it changeable and capable of development?'[1]

These issues will be approached by examining two inter-related dialectics. The first is an intellectual or 'ideological' one between the utopian proponents of reform and the realist advocates of continuing power-political practices. The second is a historical one, involving attempts to implement international order in practice, and is a dialectic between the pursuit of order and the inherent propensities towards hierarchy and dominance within the system.

As we shall see shortly, the terms of the former dialectic are much wider than those of the second: while the intellectual exploration of the issues of international order has encompassed not only reforms within the current international order but also the transformation of the current state system into something different, in practice the historical dialectic has been confined to attempts to develop regulatory diplomatic procedures and, even more narrowly, to a 'toing and froing' between 'Concert' practices and 'balance' practices among the Great Powers themselves. Nonetheless, although much more wide-ranging in its intent, the intellectual speculation about the potentiality for reform of the international order helps us to understand both the impulse to reform and its limited impact, in the actual conduct of international politics. Taking both the ideological and the historical dimensions collectively, we may accordingly distinguish a 'whig' and a 'tory' interpretation of international history, the former of which is conspicuously progressive and the latter of which is cyclical when it is not actually regressive.

In our survey of historical efforts to reform international order since 1815, the limitations of these efforts will be made apparent.

Indeed, so narrow are the confines within which this has been attempted that it becomes almost misleading to speak of 'reform of the international order'. At the very most, there have been attempts to have the Great Powers subscribe to limited 'group norms' in terms of which the powers might conduct their management of the international system; actual efforts to reform the system do not seem to have gone beyond this limited goal and, even here, as will be seen, success has been sporadic and largely non-cumulative. In fact, therefore, when we speak of historical attempts to reform the international order, we should perhaps more accurately refer to attempts to implement certain fairly minimal 'regulatory' mechanisms.[2]

The point may be made in the following way. In a discussion of the concept of international order, one writer distinguishes between two main approaches to understanding that term.[3] He considers order, first, as 'process' and, secondly, as 'substance'. According to this distinction, order in the first sense

is essentially formal in character. To satisfy this criterion a society does not have to achieve certain substantive goals or standards. Instead, the emphasis is on means rather than ends, on the manner of behaviour rather than its content, on the mode rather than the quality of life.[4]

Order, in the second sense,

is a matter not of form but of substance. It is not enough, the argument runs, for things to be done in an ordered way. It is also necessary that what is done should be such as to merit the word orderly. The essence or the effect of action is what counts not the existence of recognised processes for its execution.[5]

It would be misleading to assert that the ideological debate has been about order as substance whereas the history has been about order as process: clearly, world government could be regarded as either a substantive end or as a processual means and to that extent the distinction must break down. However, with this caveat in mind, there does seem to be some point in saying that in the history of practical attempts to reform international order, the focus has not gone beyond that of diplomatic 'processes' in an attempt to develop improved regulative systems.

The main theme of the second half of the book is, consequently, the nature of the regulatory mechanisms adopted by the powers in their inter-relationships and the attempts to 'per-

fect' these mechanisms. Unfortunately, expressing the objectives of the study even in these minimal terms is not without its own problems because there remains the danger of a further confusion.

The essence of the problem lies in trying to discern the status of these regulatory mechanisms, whether they do actively regulate the behaviour of the powers or whether they are merely the passive reflections of other processes within the system – in other words, whether we are talking about causes or about consequences. This difficulty has been usefully set out by Waltz:

> In a purely competitive economy, everyone's striving to make a profit drives the profit rate downward. Let the competition continue long enough under static conditions and everyone's profit will be zero. To infer from that condition that everyone, or anyone is seeking to minimise profit ... would obviously be absurd. And yet in international politics one frequently finds that rules inferred from the results of the inter-actions of states are prescribed to the actors and are said to be a condition of the system's maintenance.

He later continues:

> The close juxtaposition of states promotes their sameness through the disadvantages that arise from a failure to conform to successful practices. This 'sameness', an effect of the system, is often attributed to the acceptance of so-called rules of state behaviour. A possible effect of action is turned into a necessary cause in the form of a stipulated rule.[6]

Waltz's point, therefore, is that there is a genuine difficulty in discerning which 'rules' or 'norms', if any, are being observed by states and that we cannot simply deduce these rules from the resultant patterns. The problem in distinguishing, and defining, the essential characteristics of these regulatory mechanisms, which are of course nothing if not rules or norms, is as a result especially acute.

The problem is touched upon, if not satisfactorily resolved, in other writings. Keohane and Nye, for instance, discuss the same issue when they present their ideas about 'international regimes', which is alternative terminology for the regulatory mechanisms under review. Their analysis runs as follows:

> International regimes are intermediate factors between the power struc-ture of an international system and the political and economic bargain-ing that takes place within it. The structure of the system (the distri-bution of power resources among states) profoundly affects the nature of

the regime (the more or less loose set of formal and informal norms, rules and procedures relevant to the system). The regime, in turn, affects and to some extent governs the political bargaining and daily decision-making that occurs within the system.[7]

According to this formulation, the regulatory mechanisms that have characterised the international political process occupy an uncertain twilight zone somewhere between underlying power configurations and the resultant political outcomes. However, the problem of what is cause and what is effect remains and the status of these mechanisms continues to be in doubt. A study that seeks to demonstrate the history of international regulatory mechanisms in terms both of their continuities and of their evolution, is thus confronted with the very real problem of adequately capturing these mechanisms and putting them down on paper; like sand, they tend to slip through the fingers. Even where it is possible to define the essential characteristics of a system, and to distinguish it from another, the question remains whether it matters in any case, because it is unclear whether it is the 'international regimes' or the underlying power structure that, in fact, is responsible for most of the regulation that occurs.

In any event, the limited confines within which historical efforts at reforming the international order have been carried out should become abundantly clear. To the extent that international-order reform has been about the 'taming' of power politics, it has been about the minor modification of one process and its partial substitution by another. Order as substance has thus far not exercised the minds or the imagination of the world's statesmen. From this perspective, therefore, the personal preference of Arthur Burns would serve as a fair judgement upon the historical record of order-reform enterprises since 1815:

The Powers' representatives gathered in 'conversation' with each other do not as a matter of course form a community capable of an approach to the good life. But severally they can contribute to the humanising or to the depraving of the power-political process ...

If so, power-political activity should be evaluated in terms of its approach to an end – the 'humanising' of the process itself. From such a conclusion it may be thought possible to construct an ideal humanised world order. I believe that the conclusion is to be avoided, and that acts of statecraft are to be judged by the humane quality of their method and mode, and not by their tendency to produce Utopia.[8]

How, then, would we describe the 'whig' and the 'tory' interpretations of international history? The whig interpretation has two principal facets: these are, first, a conviction that progress is possible and that it has in fact occurred and, secondly, a conviction that the present is the culmination of history and that the past can be understood as sequential stages in the process of delivering us to our destination. The essentials of such a historical perspective were long since admirably set out, and criticised, by Herbert Butterfield, who argued that the whig historians had an over-riding tendency 'to emphasise certain principles of progress in the past and to produce a story which is the ratification if not the glorification of the present'.[9] He summarised in these words: 'The total result of this method is to impose a certain form upon the whole historical story, and to produce a scheme of general history which is bound to converge beautifully upon the present – all demonstrating throughout the ages the working of an obvious principle of progress.'[10]

This is not the place to enter upon a lengthy exegesis of the notion of progress and what it might mean in relation to international order, but a few comments are required. Progress has been defined as 'irreversible ameliorative change'.[11] The central question is, of course, what would constitute improvement or amelioration in the context of a discussion of international order? Some might set their sights low and aim, as Burns does, for little more than the 'humanising' of power-political processes; some might measure progress in relation to the transcendence of the present state system and its replacement by some form of centralised authority; others again might think of international order in full-blown terms as an idealised world order in which all human values are realised.

How then can a whig interpretation of 'progress' in international politics, or its tory refutation, be substantiated? One source has suggested that theories of political progress can be grouped into five categories, each of which provides a different 'end-goal' or yardstick in terms of which the occurrence of progress, or its absence, might be measured. These are listed as being: (1) a trend towards control over man's selfish or 'unsocial' nature; (2) a trend towards larger and larger political units; (3) a trend towards rational efficiency in social and political organi-

sation; (4) an advance toward greater equality; (5) an advance toward greater freedom.[12] Each of these would clearly be problematic in any political context and they are certainly so if an attempt is made to apply them to a discussion of international politics, as a cursory glance would readily indicate. The state, to the extent that it represents a 'general' interest may be thought to realise the first goal of controlling man's unsocial nature but it is itself the expression of a 'particular' interest within an international framework. As regards the second point, it is not clear whether, or in what sense, a trend towards larger political units is in itself a desirable goal or whether, in an international context, the trend toward a global political community should be encouraged merely as a contribution to the third goal, that of rational efficiency. This third, in turn, begs all kinds of questions about rationality and about the place of efficiency in the hierarchy of human values. As for the last two, the tensions between the ideals of equality and freedom have often been noted and these are aggravated at the international level where, to make the most obvious point, the equality of the lesser states can only be secured by curtailing the freedom of the larger ones.

The terms in which 'progressive' change within the international order has been affirmed and denied are, at best, uncertain and far from clear. Nonetheless, it is around these opposed interpretations that the whig and the tory schools have congregated.

The essentials of the whig interpretation have already been suggested but may be pulled together at this point. It is a progressive doctrine and argues that successive phases of international order reveal an improvement on the stage that preceded it: the League of Nations was an improvement upon the Concert of Europe and the United Nations was like-wise an improvement upon the League. Similarly, the democratic context in which foreign policy is now conducted represents an improvement upon the aristocratic context of yore and the present international order is itself preferable for that reason. Moreover, the significant aspect of international political life is not the number, and the intensity, of the wars it has experienced but rather the progressive articulation of human revulsion against these wars. In these various ways, the international order of today is assumed to be an improvement upon the international order of 1815.

The second strand of the whig interpretation is its tendency to read history 'backwards'. What is important is the present and our interest in past international practices exists only to the extent that it explains how we arrived where we now are. As Hinsley has observed 'vast efforts have been made, innumerable books have flowed, from the wish to cite Dubois or Dante, Cruce or Sully, as forerunners of the League of Nations or United Europe or the United Nations experiment.'[13] Or, as it has been expressed in one whiggish sentiment, 'the United Nations is the present manifestation of the natural legacy, passed from one generation to the next, of the continuous search for the warless world of peace and security'.[14]

According to the whig view of international history, the modern is the goal and we study history to understand the progressive unfolding of the design immanent within the historical process itself. A clear example of such reasoning can be found in the following passage, written at a time when it was difficult to maintain faith in a progressive account of the world:

The free people of the earth are today in a situation in which there is no survival for them except as United Nations. The crisis-situation is a result of historical development of the dynamism of the forces of democracy, industrial technology, and nationalism, which in mutual support and conflict have shaped the background out of which the crisis grew. But in their historical texture the possible solution of the crisis is delineated. Democracy, technology, nationalism, all point toward harmonization in the United Nations.[15]

The same author quotes the text of the resolution, for a Declaration of the Federation of the World, adopted by the Senate of the state of North Carolina in 1941 which is a classic statement of the whig profession of faith:

Just as feudalism served its purpose in human history and was superseded by nationalism, so has nationalism reached its apogee in this generation and yielded its hegemony in the body politic to internationalism. It is better for the world to be ruled by an international sovereignty of reason, social justice and peace than by diverse national sovereignties organically incapable of preventing their own dissolution by conquest.[16]

It may be worth pointing out that there are some striking resemblances between the whig interpreters of international order and the early school of 'modernisation' theory which played such a conspicuous part within the American political-science frater-

nity in the early 1960s. To the latter, the 'developing' countries of the third world were to the modern democratic state what the primitive international political system was to the one which has progressively unfolded over the past century or so. As one critic has said of the modernisation school:

Political modernity is representative democracy, and the practical achievement of the democratic ideal has reached its highest point in the United States of America. The process of modernisation, in less advanced areas of the world, is therefore very simply to be understood as one of 'transition' in which backward polities will grow increasingly to resemble the American model.[17]

In these terms, and according to the whig perspective, the international polity is but a 'developing' system writ large.

The tory interpretation stands in stark contrast to the foregoing account. Its motto, if it had one, would be *plus ça change, plus c'est la même chose.* The characteristic features of international political life are the same now as they were several centuries ago: in contrast to the emphasis upon progress, the tory belabours the theme of constancy or, if in a black mood, even gives expression to a regressive view of the world.

The spirit of the tory view is well captured in the following denunciation of the 'idealist' vision of international politics, a speech delivered at Glasgow University by F. E. Smith, First Earl of Birkenhead, in 1923:

For as long a time as the records of history have been preserved human societies passed through a ceaseless process of evolution and adjustment. This process has been sometimes pacific, but more often it has resulted from warlike disturbance. The strength of different nations, measured in terms of arms, varies from century to century. The world continues to offer glittering prizes to those who have stout hearts and sharp swords; it is therefore extremely improbable that the experience of future ages will differ in any material respect from that which has happened since the twilight of the human race.[18]

Where there are signs of change and of improvement, the tory remains convinced that this is only at the level of appearance. Underneath, the reality remains the same. Thus, as one tory has argued, when the international system of the twentieth century replaced the balance of power with a formal regulatory mechanism in the shape of a universal international organisation, all this did was to create 'power politics in disguise'.[19]

The tory interpretation has yet another twist which makes its judgement even more depressing and yields the note of regression in some of its pronouncements. The point is that, in the tory assessment, attempts to improve upon a balance system, as a form of regulatory device, not only do not realise the expectations of the whigs but can in fact be positively harmful – they lead not only to power politics in disguise but indeed to a hamstrung and inefficacious brand of power politics which leaves us with the worst of both worlds. Thus it is Hedley Bull's considered opinion that 'the attempt to apply the Grotian or solidarist formula has had the consequence not merely that the attempt to construct a superior world order is unsuccessful, but also that classical devices for the maintenance of order are weakened or undermined'.[20] In terms of this perspective, the tragedy of the inter-war period is explained not only by the failure of the League of Nations but by its hindering of the balance tactics which might otherwise have secured a fragile peace.

This is not to suggest that there is no middle ground between the two interpretations. On the contrary, most analysts prefer the safer ground in between to either of the two extremes so far presented. Inis Claude might be taken as representative of the 'agnostic' position, which sees an essential ambivalence in virtually all developments in the field of international order:

Certainly there is no guarantee that international organisation will be successful. It is easy to exaggerate the progress that has been made; supporters of international organisation are often tempted to take too seriously the ostensible gains that exist only on paper ... But it is equally easy – and perilous – to adopt a pessimism which refuses to recognise the advances that have been made and denies the hypothesis that a meaningful opportunity exists for gradual taming of power, harmonizing of interests, and building of allegiance to the ideal of a world fit for human life.[21]

The first part of the book is an elaboration of the whig and tory ideologies in relation to international order and its potential for reform. Moreover, it singles out two philosophers of the eighteenth century as representative of the two streams of thought, Kant being presented as the whig and Rousseau, however unlikely, as the tory. It is fitting that we should select two people who gave us their thoughts upon reforming the international order on the eve of the period where we take up our

historical narrative. It has been said that 'Whoever studies contemporary international relations cannot avoid hearing, behind the clash of interests and ideologies, a kind of permanent dialogue between Rousseau and Kant.'[22] To the extent that this is true, this book seeks to continue the dialogue and in its survey of the history of international order since 1815, and attempts to reform it, to suggest which of the two might be having the better of the argument.

Part I

The ideology of international order

1 *International politics and the problem of order*

The basic question to be asked is how states combine to produce a situation in international relations that we would term international order? Obviously, at one level, this is primarily a descriptive task. It involves looking at the history of international politics and discovering how international order has been created. This will be done in the latter half of the book. But equally obviously, this can only provide a partial answer, because we must first of all arrive at some conception of what is meant by international order. Moreover, such a conception is almost inevitably going to be a prescriptive one embodying certain value preferences, for the simple reason that order itself is not normatively neutral: it carries with it certain connotations and these connotations may not be acceptable to all people. What is order for the policeman may not be order for the anarchist. What is order for the bourgeoisie may not be order for a revolutionary proletariat. What is order for the Great Powers may not be order for the small ones. What is order for the satisfied states may well not be order for the dissatisfied ones. This point is familiar but still one that deserves to be made.

The book will be concerned with certain mechanisms devised, and certain norms of behaviour developed, in an effort to manage the relations between states. The mechanisms and behavioural patterns with which we will be particularly concerned include the following: the Concert of Europe, alliance systems, the League of Nations, the United Nations, bipolar alliance structures, nuclear deterrence, crisis management, spheres of influence, the economic components of international order and finally the re-emergence of a system with features resembling the more traditional balance of power. Intuitively we can appreciate that these various devices

11

and mechanisms are in some way related to the problem of international order. In fact, for the most part they are to be viewed as means towards the creation of international order. But the question is – what kind of international order? Do various order-producing systems, in fact, create different types of international order? In other words what, in a prescriptive sense, do we think the main elements of international order should be and how is this order to be attained? From this it can be seen that it is of major importance for arriving at a conception of international order that we should look at the historical pattern of efforts in this direction and examine their various consequences.

Generally speaking, we can divide approaches to international order into two categories. The distinction is implicit in the division made by two authors in their definition of such order. They see it as having two components: first, how can the likelihood of international violence be reduced; secondly, how can tolerable conditions of worldwide economic welfare, social justice and ecological stability be created?[1] In other words, how can a warless and a more just international order be achieved? Hedley Bull makes a similar distinction when he differentiates between 'minimum' and 'optimum' international order. As far as our historical survey of attempts to reform the international system is concerned, we will for the most part be discussing order in the former sense because attempts to redesign international order, in practice, have had enough difficulty in coping with the first problem without proceeding to the others.

The utility of approaching the problem of order from this twofold perspective is that it draws our attention to the fact that under many of the conditions inherent in international politics, there may be an irreconcilable contradiction between the two conceptions. A warless world may not only not be a just one, it may in fact prevent the creation of a just one. And, conversely, a just world may not only not be a peaceful one, it may in fact prevent the emergence of a peaceful one. In the last analysis the question of international order must be approached by reconciling these two facets of the problem.

Why should the problem of order present itself in such an acute form at the international level? The answer to this question requires a brief excursion into the fundamentals of the inter-

national political process and this entails locating international politics within the activity of politics as a whole.

At the risk of doing violence to a diverse and complex body of literature, it might be argued that most definitions of politics have centred around three main concepts – conflict, power and authority. Definitions that focus on the notion of conflict are concerned primarily with the conditions that give rise to the activity of politics. Definitions that focus on power are concerned primarily with the instruments by means of which the activity of politics is practised. And definitions that focus on authority are concerned primarily with what is considered to be a desirable context for the activity of politics.

The first notion starts from the basic premise that conflicts of interest are endemic in human society. This may be for the reason that the resources considered valuable by society are in short supply, because conceptions of individual happiness differ from person to person and because each in the pursuit of his material or spiritual ends is likely to be an obstacle in the path of the other's self-fulfilment. Conflict of interest is therefore ever-present in human relationships. Accordingly, as economics is concerned with the allocation and distribution of scarce resources, politics is concerned with the resolution of conflicts of interest produced by this condition of scarce resources.

The second notion, that of power, concentrates on one means by which this resolution process can be achieved. If I am stronger than you, then my conflict of interest with you can be readily resolved simply by my imposing my will upon you. It is this conception that has led to the many definitions of politics as being essentially a struggle for power. Given the existence of conflicts of interest, the only way in which an individual or a group can ensure the recognition of its own interests is by striving to improve its own power position *vis-à-vis* other individuals or groups within society. The image that this conception of politics conjures up is of the mechanical interplay of opposing forces – countervailing pressures operate against each other and the outcome will be determined by the sector that is capable of exercising the greatest pressure.

The third conception of politics, that of conciliation through authoritative procedures, like the second one is concerned with

the process by means of which conflict of interest can be resolved. But unlike the second conception, it stresses not the uncontrolled interplay of forces but rather the resolution of conflicts via regulated procedures. Its key concept, if you like, is authority rather than naked power. It is concerned with the devising of legitimate procedures. In the democratic context, the distinction between these second and third notions of politics is conveyed in the dictum about the counting of heads rather than the breaking of them. There is still a contest but this contest is circumscribed within defined limits.

On this basis, how are we to provide a more specific identification of the precise nature of the international political process? Which of the three conceptions of politics, if any, most closely resembles the core of international political life?

One way of attempting to do this is to compare the salient characteristics of international politics with those of any domestic political system. By displaying what is unique about the international political system, we may better understand the precise nature of the political problems confronted at the international level. The points about to be made are, of course, something of a simplification. In making these distinctions between domestic and international politics, I will exaggerate the differences for the purposes of initial presentation.

What then are the main differences between domestic and international politics? There are at least four points that are usually made in the text-books and they may be worth repeating at this stage. They are:

(1) First, unlike most domestic political systems, the international system has no final repository of decision-making authority. This point can actually be expressed in several ways. Unlike most domestic systems, there is no central body, no government if you like, that is the final arbiter in disputes between its constituent units. The international political system is a decentralised one, in which the units are sovereign or autonomous. There is no ultimate authority to which they are subordinate. It has been claimed that this is the most basic fact of international life, the fact that endows the subject with its unique characteristics. Furthermore, it has been contended that this facet of international life makes states operate in

accordance with political rules that are quite different from those found in domestic systems. It is, therefore, this point that forms the basis of the claim that international politics, as a branch of knowledge, constitutes an autonomous discipline.

(2) The second point is directly related to the first. As we have just said, it is one of the defining characteristics of domestic politics that they take place within a context of the existence of an ultimate decision-making authority, the government, and that this distinguishes domestic from international politics. It is also one of the defining characteristics of domestic politics that they take place in the context of the existence of a body, again the government, that possesses a monopoly over the legitimate use of force. This does not mean that there are never challenges to this authority and that groups within a national society will not sometimes resort to force in order to further their aims. However, the authority of the state is generally recognised and as a consequence of this authority it is legitimate for the state to employ force in order to defend itself against internal or external challenges. This provides another point of contrast with the international situation. There is no single body which possesses a monopoly over the legitimate use of force. Each state, because it considers itself to be sovereign, feels entitled to employ its own national forces whenever it deems it necessary. Thus whereas private resort to force constitutes the exception in domestic politics and occurs only when the authority of the state is no longer recognised by some sector within it, there is no such inhibition on the use of force at the international level and consequently resort to violence has constituted the rule rather than the exception.

(3) The third point of difference helps to explain why the first two differences exist. Most domestic political systems are founded on some sort of society-wide consensus. This consensus may only be a very tenuous one based, for instance, on a common nationality. It may not even be a spontaneous consensus but may have had its origins in subjection to the rule of force. But whatever the basis of consensus, there is some community of values throughout the system that makes the functioning of a centralised political authority possible. It is doubtful whether any such consensus or community of values

exists at the international level. Although there are some states that embrace a wide variety of ethnic and racial groups, there is no political system as heterogeneous as the international one. The diversity in social, economic, religious and ethnic terms makes subordination to a common political authority at the international level a vastly greater problem than at the state level.

(4) The fourth point of difference has been implicit in much of what has already been said. Whereas in domestic political systems the actors, the units involved in the political process, are individual people, this is not the case with the international system. Admittedly, individuals are not the only political actors on the domestic scene. People organise themselves into groups that are crucial actors in the political process. But compared with the international scene, as a matter of emphasis, there is a difference because the most important actors at the international level are essentially legal fictions. Clearly all the actions and all the decisions taken in the name of a state are taken by people. But by adding the phrase 'in the name of the state' you are making an important comment on the nature of these actions or decisions. What you are confronted with are actions and decisions that are said to be representative of vast political collectivities, namely states. And it may well be the case that the political behaviour of vast organisations will differ from the political behaviour of individuals: it may even differ from the behaviour of the individuals who in fact constitute the organisation. The point of distinction is as follows: the political system of a state is the arena within which various interests, some in conflict, some in harmony, compete and coalesce. But if you imagine the international political system on the same lines as a domestic one, you have a much more complex picture, because the actors – the states – that are competing for the advancement of their own interests are in fact not bodies with single interests but bodies that are already aggregations of competing interests.

If we now move on to study the means by which these conflicts of interest are resolved, this can be done conveniently by recalling the two resolution models that were referred to above, the power model and the authority model. The first was described as

the unbridled interplay of opposing forces. The second was described as being characterised by the pursuit of decision-making procedures, the legitimacy of which would be recognised by the constituent units. All international political practice can be encompassed within these two extremes and a major point of interest for the student of international politics is, which tendency is uppermost or, historically speaking, how have the two tendencies been combined?

How then are decisions made within the international political system? First let us look at the various practices that would fall within the first model, the power model. Here we can distinguish a continuum of practices that begins with diplomacy and bargaining and ends with outright violence. Diplomacy and bargaining is to international politics what the free market is to economics. Every state sets out to obtain the best deal for itself and its success or lack of it in this effort is largely determined by the resources that it commands. Given the characteristic features of the international system that we described above, this is perhaps the most distinctive political technique at the international level. Since no authority is in a position to arbitrate between two competing states, the political process is essentially a test of wills and capabilities.

Which other international activities would be embraced within the power model? Well, clearly the actual use of force. This surely is the ultimate example of the essentially power-based nature of the international political process. In the absence of common political authority, and if states cannot be persuaded to conciliate for prudential reasons, then ultimately force must be the arbiter between competing states. In fact, starting from the premise of the decentralised or anarchic nature of international life, and of the prominent place that this accords to violence as the *ultima ratio*, some people have argued that the subject matter of international politics is no more and no less than the study of war. This view should not be accepted. The study of war is certainly an extremely important part of the discipline but it is not coextensive with the field of international politics as a whole. The study of international politics centres on the consequences of the type of political organisation into which the world is arranged. War is undoubtedly the most dramatic of these consequences – it

is the extreme manifestation of the decentralised nature of the international political system. But it is not the only consequence with which we are concerned because, although it might be the ultimate form of conflict resolution, it is not the only such technique that has been developed.

Diplomacy, bargaining and war have been mentioned as belonging within the power model of international politics. But there is yet another practice that should be included within this category and that is the tacit use of force, which can be employed by states that have a preponderance of power. This can be illustrated with an example. There is good reason for thinking that there is emerging a serious conflict of interest between the industrialised countries of the northern hemisphere and the developing countries of the third world – the rich and the poor nations. There are at least three ways in which this conflict could be resolved. On the model of a domestic political system, there could be political activity on the part of the poor states in order to obtain a redistribution of income within the system as a whole. But clearly no political authority exists at the moment that would effect such a redistribution. The second method would be the use of violence on the part of the poor states to force such a redistribution, something that is not as yet a very strong possibility. But there is a third means by which this conflict of interest can be resolved and this is the way in which it is, in fact, being resolved at the moment. This is for the conflict to be resolved in the interests of the stronger party. The economic *status quo* at the moment favours the industrialised countries. And the industrialised countries can maintain this *status quo* by doing nothing at all because their position is backed up by tacit force. So the point is this: decisions at the international level are sometimes made by the application of force and the eruption of violence, but we should not be blind to the many decisions, or non-decisions, that are made by those more powerful parties who do not actually have to employ their force but can keep it tacitly in the background.

These are some aspects of international politics that fall within the power model. But there is another side to the story, which should not be ignored. If the basic fact of international life is its decentralised political structure, then what we should be looking

at is not only the logical consequences of this fact (the prevalence of war) but the steps that have been taken to try to counteract or overcome this fact of decentralisation. This entails the whole history of efforts to establish procedures, techniques, institutions that might compensate for the absence of a supreme decision-making body within the international system. It is the search for some such procedures or institutions that constitutes the most interesting theme of modern international history, as is the manner in which the search for these procedures and institutions has been combined with the practices that we have described as falling within the power model. It is the tension, the conflict, the uneasy harmony between the power model of politics and the authority model of politics that provides the fascination in the study of international politics.

The central preoccupation of most of the attempts at creating international order has been the role of force in international politics. In fact, the major approaches to developing inter-national order can be classified according to the attitude that they hold to the question of force in international affairs. From this perspective, we can construct a threefold category of ap-proaches to creating what has been called 'minimum' inter-national order on the basis of the relationship between the mechanism and force. The three categories of international order would accordingly be the following: (1) international order through the recognition of the role of force and through its utilisation; (2) international order through placing constraints on the use of force; (3) and finally, international order through the eventual rejection of the special place which force has in inter-national politics. Each of these will be elaborated upon in turn.

(1) First, we may consider those theories that recognise the use of force and seek to utilise it for the creation of order. Here two schools of thought can be specified, although the second one should, perhaps, more accurately be regarded as a specific manifestation of the first. Obviously what is being referred to here is the school of thought associated with the balance of power. There are two aspects of this doctrine that are relevant to the problem of international order. The first is that the doctrine accepts the state unit and its proclivity to employ violence as the realistic basis upon which order must be

created. What is meant by order according to this theory is such things as equilibrium or stability. Threats to order would be those attempts to overthrow the system and create pre-ponderance. In other words, this theory seeks not to change the fact of the power potential of the individual states but rather to use this fact in the pursuit of order. No attempt is made to curb the power potential of the individual states. Rather the power of the one is turned against that of the other, thereby producing equilibrium. It is in this sense that balance of power recognises the realities of the situation and attempts not to change them but to utilise them for its own ends.

The second feature of balance of power to be considered is its attitude to the use of force. The point here is that although for the most part balance of power as theory can be regarded as a means to international order through conflict control, the theory nonetheless makes allowance for violence. This is to say that within the framework of balance of power, order and violence are not entirely incompatible. On the contrary, as a last resort, violence may be the only means of maintaining order. Because order is defined in terms of the stability and the preservation of the state system, a threat to this system can be met by violence and this response would be regarded as order-producing rather than order-destroying. It can, therefore, be seen that balance of power is the theory which seeks least to change the reality of international politics; although order for the most part is pro-duced by controlled force-manipulation, in certain circumstances order can be preserved by direct force-utilisation.

The second school of thought in this section is the school of nuclear deterrence and, as was said, this is merely a subset of the general balance-of-power school. A major difference between the two, however, is that although the former permits force manipu-lation in the interest of order, it would nonetheless regard force utilisation in the nuclear sense as incompatible with order. Otherwise the positions are very similar. The argument of the strategists would run as follows. In nuclear deterrence, we have a system that displays all the realistic merits of the balance of power but removes from the balance of power its one serious defect. It makes realistic use of force by accepting its existence but seeks to neutralise it by balancing force against force.

This much traditional balance of power also did. But the additional virtue of deterrence is that this neutralisation is so strong that no attempt to disrupt the balance is ever likely to occur. Because of this there will never be any need to maintain equilibrium by violent means. Order is therefore maintained by a protracted stalemate. We thus have the paradox that nuclear weapons, the greatest single threat to the continuation of the human species, are regarded by many as the best possible guarantee of peace and order currently available to the actors in the international system.

It is at this point that there is a danger of the classification, herein presented, breaking down. We have placed nuclear deterrence within the category where the fact of force is recognised and made use of. At the same time, we can see that it might also fit into the second category of the placing of constraints on the use of force because the nature of the weapons is surely a powerful constraint in its own right. Nonetheless, the order that is produced is, just as in the balance-of-power situation, the product of the natural interplay of forces rather than the product of deliberate intervention by means of some device or other. There is no consciously constructed mechanism that would constrain the use of force. To this extent, nuclear deterrence represents a *laissez-faire* situation in which order in the last resort depends on the free interplay of competing forces. To the extent that there are constraints on the use of force built into the system, they are no more than an extension of the cost-benefit analysis of the value of using force that existed in the traditional balance situation as well. There is no constraint of a legal, institutional or physical nature.

(2) Within this second category – of order produced by constraints on the use of force – we would include such devices as collective security, arms control and the development of international law. What these three mechanisms have in common is a shared realisation that the major problem of order is that of the sovereign right of the state to resort to war, and what each of these devices seeks to do is to place – respectively – an institutional, a physical and a legal constraint on the use of that force. As in the ideas put forward in category one, force is seen to be the basic cause of the problem but while the theories in

category one argue that force, in one form or another, is also the solution, those in category two contend that the only solution is to change the rules of the game with respect to the utilisation of violence by states.

According to collective security, the major threat to order is one which would allow the use of violence against the interests of the international community as a whole. For that reason, the balance of power is to be institutionalised. This will have, according to the supporters of the theory, two beneficial results. First, it will make the balance of power more effective and there will be less chance of a preponderant power emerging. But also it will ensure that violence, if used, is always used in a legitimate manner. Since power is vested in the international community, that power will not be abused in the way it had been by individual nation states.

Arms control starts from similar premises, namely that the nature of the international system is such that violent conflicts between states are an inevitable concomitant of the system. It too accepts the system but tries to limit the resulting violence by placing constraints on the capabilities of the states. It does not seek to improve the states or the system within which they operate. In fact, it displays the same intellectual subtlety to the problem of war as do suggestions that castration might solve the problem of rape. Arms control, or disarmament, relies upon military castration in the sense that, even if it will not deprive the states of their basic urges, it will at least deprive them of the means of gratification.

Arms control, however, suffers from a further internal inconsistency, which might best be described in the following manner. We can conceive of war in many ways, Clausewitz's notion of war as a political instrument probably being the most famous. However, two other conceptions might be introduced because they help to illustrate the tension within the arms-control camp. We will label these the pathological and the cataclysmic conceptions of war. The pathological relates, of course, to the study of diseases. What is meant by this is that the relationship between war and international society should be regarded as analogous to the relationship between disease and health. According to this conception, it is assumed that health is the normal condition of

the international system; i.e. the normal characteristic of the international system is co-operation and non-violent conflict resolution. When a war occurs this represents a disease of the international body politic, an affliction which must be removed so that international society may be restored, to its previous condition of health. As you can see, this conception of war incorporates a value-judgement within it – that peace is the norm and war constitutes a deviant case. It is also to be regarded as an affliction that is imposed from the outside. Which is to say that it is different from the accidental view of war in that war is produced not by man's failings alone but by the intervention, if you like, of a malevolent Nature. War, like disease, is a scourge of nature, it is not something that man inflicts upon himself. Secondly, and employing Rapoport's term,[2] we can conceive of war as a cataclysm. In many respects, this category is virtually identical with the previous one. The idea is that war is regarded as being analogous to a natural disaster of some kind, say a cyclone or an earthquake. Once again, as in the previous instance, this suggests an aberration from the norm and it also suggests an affliction from the outside. Wars, like natural disasters, do not represent a human failing: they are something that nature imposes upon humanity.

Nonetheless, despite the similarities in these two conceptions, there is an important difference in the recommendations they make in relation to war, which arises precisely from their respective analyses of the nature of the problem to be tackled. The pathological view that regards war as a disease follows the medical tradition that diseases are curable. We have to understand their causes scientifically and then we will be in a position to take remedial action: international society can be restored to health. This is clearly not applicable in the case of the cataclysmic interpretation. This works on the assumption that no matter how perfect our scientific understanding of natural disasters such as earthquakes, we still cannot cure them. The most that we can do is take preventive action, which will not stop these occurrences but will minimise the damage that will result from them.

Obviously, this distinction is not just an academic one but one that could have important practical implications. For anyone engaged in devising a country's foreign or defence policy, it

naturally makes all the difference in the world whether he thinks war can be prevented altogether or whether the best that can be done is to limit the resulting damage. Let us take a concrete demonstration of this problem. If we start off with the premise shared by both the pathological and the cataclysmic views that war is a scourge, we can agree that we would like to avoid wars and we might agree, as has historically been the case, that an important contribution to this end can be made via arms control. But the problem with arms control is that there may be more than one purpose behind it: you may undertake it with the intention of avoiding war altogether – in accordance with the pathological view you might argue that disarmament is a cure for war that will eliminate it; alternatively, you might agree to an arms-control programme with the intention of limiting the amount of damage that would result from a future war. If both sides only have ten missiles, then there will be less damage than if they had a hundred apiece. This, then, would be the cataclysmic recommendation that we take measures to reduce the impact of future disasters.

Unfortunately, these two goals of disarmament, flowing from different assessments of the problem, can be in conflict with each other. Clearly, if we were to be guided by the second objective of disarmament, that of damage limitation in the event of war, this could undermine the first objective, that of preventing war: if we reduced the number of missiles each side had in order to reduce future damage, this could have the unfortunate side-effect of actually increasing the likelihood of war breaking out, precisely for the reason that if you reduce the likely damage of future wars, you reduce the fear of war and to that extent you may undercut the deterrence upon which the avoidance of war is based. Whereas if you try to strengthen deterrence, by reducing damage-limiting capabilities, you in fact ensure that in the event of war, the maximum amount of damage will be realised.

Lastly, within this second category of imposing constraints upon the use of force, something must be said about international law. It is perhaps a truism but there was of course virtually no such thing as international law before the sixteenth or seventeenth centuries for the simple reason that there were no inde-

pendent national units whose relations required regulation by such a body of law. Which is one way of saying that international law arose simultaneously with the emergence of the European international system. Which again, in turn, is one way of saying that international law developed simultaneously with the conception of political sovereignty. It required the disintegration of the mediaeval ideal that all Europe constituted a political and religious whole, subject to Emperor and Pope respectively, before there was any felt need to promulgate a body of rules according to which the newly emerging political units of Europe would conduct themselves. In other words, international law was no more than the obverse side of the emerging doctrine of sovereignty.

For that reason, there is a tension within international law because it is, on the one hand, a reinforcement of national sovereignty and, on the other, it is intended to be a constraint upon that sovereignty. We might highlight this duality by speaking of a 'utopian' and a 'realist' interpretation of the role of international law.

How should we characterise the essential difference between the utopian and the realist positions on international law with respect to the duality between sovereignty-reducing and sovereignty-reinforcing aspects? Take an illustration. Some commentators on the American constitution argue that there are two things we can learn from the study of that constitution. On the one hand, the constitution contains the basic rules of the game: it describes the respective powers of the various organs of government and lays down the moves that the various players – the presidency, Congress, the judiciary – may make. So the most basic function of the constitution is to serve as a rule-book. But studying the constitution tells you something more than this. It not only tells you the rules of the game, it also gives you a fairly accurate reflection of the state of play. If you look at the way in which articles of the constitution have been interpreted by the Supreme Court or at the specific amendments to the constitution, this gives you some idea of the present distribution of power between the various branches of government – for instance, you might say that the run of play was favouring federal as opposed to state powers, favouring the executive

as against Congress. In any case, the point is that the constitution, although it is essentially a rule-book, may also from another angle be regarded as a score-card as well.

These two perspectives on the constitution capture the essence of the respective positions of the utopian and the realist. For the utopian, international law is a body of rules that will govern the processes of international politics. For the realist, international law does little more than reflect the state of international political play. As a case in point, there is the widespread argument that international law has been basically European law, an outgrowth of the European state system. As such, many aspects of it have been found objectionable by the emerging third-world states who regard it as an instrument that both reflects and perpetuates the dominant position of the western powers within international society. For instance, from the point of view of the Australian aboriginal, the international law that permitted Australia to be acquired in the name of the British Crown was not an objective body of rules. It is seen very much as an instrument that facilitated the realisation of the interests of the dominant powers at the time, i.e. the expanding European states.

(3) The third category of minimum international order is those solutions that advocate the reform of the system in such a way that the problem of force is solved by making it disappear. This includes the various theories of world government that argue that the main obstacle to international order is the anarchy between the individual states and that, consequently, the only way to remove the anarchy is to destroy the units that produce it, namely the states.

There is an influential tradition of thought, concerned with reform of the state system, that self-consciously employs the model of the domestic political system as the basis for its solution to the problem of international order. It is assumed that government at the national level has been successful in solving the problem of order and that, by extension, we can eliminate war from international life by setting up some form of world government. A lucid description of this approach can be found elsewhere:

One of the chief intellectual supports of this doctrine is what may be called the domestic analogy, the argument from the experience of

individual men in domestic society to the experience of states, according to which the need of individual men to stand in awe of a common power in order to live in peace is a ground for holding that states must do the same. The conditions of an orderly social life, on this view, are the same among states as they are within them: they require that the institutions of domestic society be reproduced on a universal scale.[3]

The argument relies heavily upon social-contract imagery. Order is established at the national level by a social contract whereby people submit to a common authority, the better to protect their lives and liberties. Accordingly, just as men used to live in a state of nature, so the states now live in a state of nature *vis-à-vis* each other. The solution, therefore, is a further social contract whereby the states give up their absolute freedom to a common authority.

This approach to issues of international order has a long heritage in western thought. When it is remembered that Europe throughout the mediaeval period had been regarded as a unity, whether in its religious or its imperial aspects, it is not surprising that those who were witnessing the emergence of a state system dominated by sovereign, independent states should have recalled that earlier period of European unity and should have regarded a supra-national entity as the natural solution to international anarchy and war. If it is true that man never recovers from the shock of leaving the womb, then this seems also to have been the case with the states of Europe.

It is now necessary to return to the discussion of the problem of order at the international level. The basic problem is that of effecting political change within the system. In most domestic societies this task is accomplished because there are institutions – such as electoral procedures – that allow for the expression of grievances and thus make the system aware of needs for change and sometimes, although not always, facilitate the initiation of change. The international system obviously does not have any such procedures or institutions that command total authority. The result is that the major deficiency of the international system is its inability as yet to devise any universally acceptable means for permitting peaceful change.

This elementary point has been repeated for the simple reason that the basic condition of international politics relates directly to

the problem of the nature of international order and the type of international order that is acceptable. The international system has as yet not managed to devise a universally acceptable means for the peaceful resolution of conflict brought about by change within the system. However, in this chapter we have been considering various international devices and mechanisms that have as their basic premise the doctrine that order is to be attained by either deflecting or constraining or eliminating the element of force in international politics. The major implication of the whole train of thought embodied in these various solutions is that international order is achieved by the control of violent conflict. But if violent change is not to be permitted and the system as yet has not developed institutions for the accommodation of interests on a peaceful basis, how are conflicts of interest, and especially those induced by change, to be effected? Or does order require the complete ossification of the system, one in which no change is possible and order becomes no more than a synonym for the preservation of the *status quo*? Clearly this is neither a realistic nor a desirable alternative. If not, in what way can we arrive at a conception of international order that makes allowance for change in cases where this change is likely to be resisted? This is a problem that is common to all political systems but it is brought out especially clearly in the international case because of the peculiar qualities of that system.

Posing the question in this form, should make us aware of the difficulties in the path of a definition of what we have termed minimum international order, because if we equate this minimum order with the prevention of violence then we must assume, given that there is not an absolute harmony of interests at the international level – a reasonable assumption – that this type of 'negative' order is going to be in the interests of certain sectors of international society and is going to affect adversely the interests of certain other sectors. A moment's reflection on the various mechanisms for promoting order that will be examined in this book would appear to confirm this conclusion.

First of all, consider the balance of power. As its very name implies, this is a system of order that derives its motive force from the fact of power. There is order for those states that are in a position to counterbalance power by power, the Great Powers. Con-

sequently, as Modelski has observed, 'I regard order-keeping as a function assumed and performed in recent historical experience by the great powers and by the diplomatic and strategic complex associated with them.'[4] From the viewpoint of the lesser powers, the order is uncertain, depending upon a volatile balance that they themselves cannot control.

At the same time, one virtue of the balance of power is that it does not discriminate against change for its own sake. The only requirement is that change, if it is to be brought about, must be accompanied by adequate power: change comes about as soon as there is a margin of power on its side.

The League of Nations too instituted its own brand of international order. It, too, perpetuated the division into large and small states and although it made concessions to the small states, it would be difficult to deny that it produced an order sustained by, and largely in the interests of, the Great Powers. It was also to produce a striking example of international order being harnessed to the requirements of the existing *status quo*. The order that was produced at Versailles was one that was overwhelmingly in the interests of the victor nations. It perpetuated a sharp division between the victors and the vanquished, between the 'have' and the 'have not' states. Because of the inbuilt bias of the inter-war international order, this was one that could not adjust peacefully to change.

This example very clearly demonstrates the principle that most international orders have been in the interests of some states but not of others. The best example of this is the situation where the international order has been named after one particular state that has exercised commanding influence over the system as a whole. Thus we have had the so-called Pax Romana, Pax Britannica, and Pax Americana, and currently some people fear a Pax Sovietica. The League of Nations was conspicuously a Pax of this nature.

The post-1945 period has not witnessed any striking modifications in this respect. We could point to the United Nations Security Council and say with justification that the order inaugurated in 1945 was one overwhelmingly in favour of the major powers. It imposed a system of collective security in which order would be enforced upon the smaller states if they resorted

to violence, but because of the veto the same constraints could not be imposed upon the Great Powers.

Moving outside the ambit of the United Nations and looking at the basic reality of the post-war power configuration, we could say even more precisely that the order that has been established is one dictated by, and in the interests of, the two Super-Powers. It is they who command the nuclear deterrent that plays such a major role in the maintenance of the present international order. It is in their interest that many regional disputes have been frozen. Because the Super-Powers have become involved in almost all regions of the globe, and usually on competing sides, the solution of regional disputes that would normally have been accomplished by traditional military means has been prevented. It has become too dangerous, in many cases, to have these disputes resolved because it might lead to a confrontation between the Super-Powers.

There is another sense in which the present international order is one suited to the interests of the Super-Powers. Most of the conceptions of order that have been considered thus far have been based on an understanding that the state has the only legitimate monopoly of violence within the system. That is to say that central to the very idea of order has been a recognition of the sovereignty of the state in matters of its own jurisdiction. Just how central this notion of state sovereignty and state monopoly of violence has been in the development of the international system can be seen with reference to the numerous complaints that the emergence of trans-national terrorist groups as international actors, capable of resorting to large-scale violence, constitutes a major threat to world order. In accordance with the traditional image, only states should exercise this right of violence.

In essence, then, the problem with the notion of 'minimum' international order is that, in the absence of alternative means of securing change, attempts to predicate order upon the control of violence inevitably introduce disequilibria into the system. More so than anything, it has been the pursuit of order in this sense that has reinforced the hierarchical dimensions of international society.

2   *Kant and the tradition of optimism*

This chapter and the succeeding one are concerned with the respective traditions of optimism and pessimism in relation to the international order, the former asserting that reform is both necessary and possible and the latter that reform is both un-attainable and dangerous. For reasons of convenience, and in accordance with widespread practice, we may refer to these traditions as those of utopianism and realism. By way of caution, however, it should be pointed out that although there is extensive overlap between optimism and pessimism, on the one hand, and utopianism and realism, on the other, the two are not absolutely identical. Optimism reflects a faith that progressive change is possible, whereas utopianism, in its strict sense, pertains to the pursuit of the unattainable ideal. Likewise, pessimism is a denial of the possibility of progress, whereas realism, again in its strict sense, means the harmonious blending of practical activities with an extant reality without necessarily asserting that reality is itself unchanging. Nonetheless, for present purposes, we shall refer to utopianism as the ideological impetus to reform of the inter-national order and to realism as the main source of resistance.

During the 1950s and 1960s, utopian thought, like ideology generally, was deemed to be at an end. Typically, Judith Shklar pronounced that 'the urge to construct grand designs for the political future of mankind is gone', basing her judgement on the ground that 'the last vestiges of utopian faith required for such an enterprise have vanished'.[1] Even more recently, and correspond-ingly less perspicaciously, Paul Seabury expressed the view that 'a utopian concern for "world order" as a planned qualitative transformation designed to meet new needs seems to have been washed out ... Prescriptive futurism now seems passé.'[2] In the event, such obituaries have turned out to be premature: thought about international-order reform has experienced a resurgence during the 1970s, to such an extent that we might be tempted to

equate the intellectual mood of the present time with the utopian impulse of the post-1918 decade.[3]

This prompts the question: is there anything novel in the form of utopian speculation about international order that has emerged in the 1970s or is the phenomenon better understood as part of that longer tradition of reformist thought that has characterised the history of intellectual endeavour ever since the inception of the European states system? Or, to put the question more incisively, can the current *genre* of utopian writing avoid Hinsley's bitter indictment of twentieth-century 'peace projects', namely that 'every scheme for the elimination of war that men have advocated since 1917 has been nothing but a copy or an elaboration of some seventeenth-century programme – as the seventeenth-century programmes were copies of still earlier schemes'[4]? Are current ideas concerning international-order reform as totally atavistic as Hinsley suggests, or do the 1970s constitute a watershed in this form of intellectual enterprise?

It is to this question that the present chapter addresses itself. However, the delimitations of the exercise should first be specified. It is not the intention of this survey to consider the novelty, or otherwise, of recent utopian writing in terms of its 'preferred solutions' or in terms of the details of its 'preferred world orders'. The 'instrumental' aspects of ideas about international-order reform have been classified elsewhere on the basis of three distinct orientations: political–structural, functional and universal–cultural approaches to reform, all of which highlight the particular 'instrument' or 'process' of reform itself, or focus on the 'end-goal' when it is realised.[5] However, this chapter is not concerned with 'solutions'. Virtually every survey of 'peace projects' or of the history of ideas concerning international-order reform has been preoccupied with the details of these 'solutions' and has been so at the expense of a more general appreciation of the continuities and discontinuities in utopian thought that stem from the structure of their arguments about the need for reform, irrespective of their preferred variant for its attainment. It is with the logical structures of utopian thought that we are concerned and within these confines that the novelty of present utopian thought will be assessed. In other words, the focus is upon the mainsprings of utopianism, on why it believes that 'solutions' are possible, or, indeed, necessary.

THE NATURE OF UTOPIANISM

What is conveyed by the term 'utopian thought' is also in need of some initial elaboration. In terms of a recent classification of patterns of thought about the future, the utopian tradition with which we are concerned falls unequivocally into the natural–rational category.[6] Such an approach is, according to Cox, 'founded on the concept of a duality distinguishing the inward nature from the outward appearance of human institutions and events' and one of the lines of inquiry stemming from it is 'the normative task of designing polities consistent with the rational nature of man'.[7]

More generally, it can be argued that there are four inter-related distinguishing marks of utopianism, four characteristics of such thought, which inhere, to a greater or lesser degree, in all its variants. The first of these is a belief in 'progress'. As one writer has expressed it 'the utopian faith asserts that human nature can be understood in terms not of immutable facts but of poten-tialities which are progressively actualized in the course of his-tory'.[8] Indeed, Hedley Bull has argued that this belief in progress was the distinctive attribute of the post-1918 generation of 'idealists'.

The distinctive characteristic of these writers was their belief in progress: the belief, in particular, that the system of international relations that had given rise to the First World War was capable of being transformed . . .; that . . . it was in fact being transformed; and that their responsibility as students of international relations was to assist this march of progress.[9]

Utopians are, therefore, concerned to promote improvement and because of this it might be said that utopian thought is, in the loosest sense of the word, 'revolutionary' or, in Mannheim's phraseology, 'the explosive material for bursting the limits of the existing order'.[10]

The second element is logically related to the first: it follows from this belief in progress that utopians share an essentially non-deterministic view of the world. The belief in progress would, in itself, be meaningless were it not predicated upon a similar faith in the efficacy of change through human agency. This faith, in turn, derives from a particular view of the nature of the historical process.[11] Accordingly, the distinctive 'realist' and 'utopian' views of historical motion might be crudely depicted in the following

terms: unlike the 'realist', who considers the driving force of history to be located in antecedent causes that push the process along, the utopian makes allowance for the power of the idea of the future that, to some extent, is able to pull the process along.

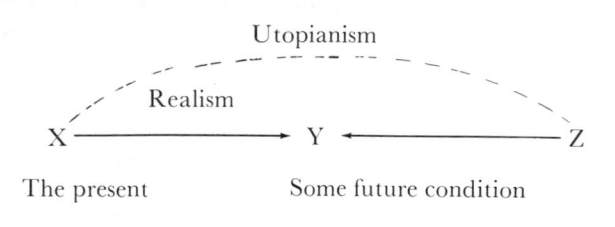

Utopianism

Realism

X ———————→ Y ←——————— Z

The present   Some future condition

This may be represented figuratively (see diagram). For the realist, the transition from x to y is determined by the total condition of x itself; for the utopian, the transition to y can be effected, to some degree, by having a conception of the future goal z. The former emphasises the 'push from behind'; the latter introduces the notion of a 'pull from in front' and it is in this way that human agency becomes effective in inducing change.

The third characteristic of utopian thought is its pervasive rationalism. As one analyst of utopianism has argued, it believes that 'a rational and moral political order can be imposed on the international system' and that 'just as individual men are good and rational, so too states are capable of behaving in a moral and rational manner towards one another'.[12] Indeed, when utopians speak about 'progress', they invariably mean by it the actualisation of man's potential for rationality.

The pervasiveness of this belief is easily demonstrated. Perhaps the classic example is to be found in the writings of Norman Angell, early in this century. In *The Great Illusion* (1909) Angell argued that wars were not financially profitable and his messianic message was that it remained only to convince statesmen of this fact in order to liberate mankind from the scourge of war. Likewise, more than a century earlier, Bentham had subscribed to the notion of a rationalist universe: 'Between the interests of nations there is nowhere any real conflict; if they appear repugnant anywhere it is only in proportion as they are misunderstood.'[13] Like Angell, Bentham was convinced that the calamities of international politics were no more than instances in the failure of comprehension.

In this sense, the faith in rationality draws attention to the affinities between utopian thought and the mediaeval natural-law tradition. This tradition assumes that there are objective rules governing the universe and that man, through the use of right reason, can deduce what these rules of behaviour are. Above all, it was a part of the natural-law tradition that the elements of justice could be objectively known. Accordingly the post-World War One generation of utopians believed that men, acting rationally, would also be acting in accordance with the dictates of justice: standards of justice were knowable by right reasoning. This came through powerfully in the theoretical underpinnings of the League of Nations. As Lord Robert Cecil, one of the most prominent British sponsors of the League, was to write in condemnation of the old system of the balance of power, to which the League was seen as a corrective, 'there is this fatal objection to the system of international anarchy. It makes justice and right dependent on the fortunes of war.'[14] Now, if war is not to determine what is just, what else can? By implication, Cecil evidently assumes that there is an objective standard of justice to which all men, regardless of nationality, will subscribe.

The belief in rationality has its obverse side in the fourth predominant characteristic of utopian thought – the assumption of a natural harmony of interests.[15] Accordingly, the interests of states are taken to be complementary rather than antagonistic and the game of international politics is mixed-motive rather than zero-sum. The 'invisible hand' ensures a happy outcome for everyone because basic interests can be reconciled and are not mutually exclusive. Only, indeed, if such were the case would it be possible for principles of rationality to exercise their sway. Symptomatic of the centrality of this belief to the utopian position were the execrations heaped by the inter-war idealist, Alfred Zimmern, upon the 'wicked theory of the mutual incompatibility of nations'.[16]

A CURRENT WATERSHED?

We may take these four components as the irreducible minimum of any utopian position and, as such, it can be assumed that they are as much an integral part of current plans for world-order reform as of any other age. On what bases, then, might rest the

claim that we have reached a watershed in utopian thought? A survey of the literature reveals that current utopian prescriptions appear self-consciously aware of their novelty and it is possible to distinguish several grounds upon which the claim is advanced. Four such grounds are recurrent in the literature:

(1) The first emphasises the generally greater sophistication of present research into alternative world-orders. This itself might be said to be contingent upon the development of social-science techniques and methodologies. This contention is to be found in its most explicit form in Beres and Targ: 'Until now, the long tradition of social thought concerning alternative world futures has placed little or no emphasis on the essential methodological underpinnings of inquiry.'[17]

(2) Closely related to this, and in some cases identical to it, is the claim that current thought is devoted not only to the specification of end-goals but equally if not more importantly to the detailed explication of 'transition strategies', not only with 'preferred world orders' but also with how to get there.[18] By way of analogy, in their own self-estimation, the current utopians have done for world-order reform what Marx claimed to have done for utopian socialism.

(3) Current order-reform projects have also been deemed to be *sui generis* on the basis of the global scope of the problems they are designed to counteract. This is the theme of Richard Falk's writings, that 'we are living now in the first stages of a planetary crisis' and that 'it is the first such known crisis in the history of the planet'.[19] In a similar vein, Camilleri has prognosticated that 'in order to sustain the organic evolution of the human species, it will be necessary to develop perspectives and responses that are both radical and global in inspiration'.[20]

(4) Lastly, and derivative from the nature of the problems it is intended to overcome, current utopian writing has been distinguished on the basis of its broader platform – that it is concerned not simply with the realisation of the value of peace but with the attainment of other values as well. WOMP, for instance, has specified its areas of concern as those of war, poverty, racial oppression, environmental decay and alienation and it has been contended that this distinguishes present efforts from the purely war-oriented writings of earlier generations of

utopians. In a sense, it might also be said that this broadening out of the goals of utopian reform has taken place *pari passu* with a shift of focus from the tribulations of *international* order to the issues of *world* order as such.[21] At any rate, Rosen and Jones are no doubt correct when they observe that 'war–peace issues no longer monopolize scholarly examination of the future'.[22]

Do these various contentions, individually or collectively, amount to a persuasive case for regarding current utopian literature as a significantly novel intellectual departure? How valid is the judgement of one writer who, in comparing the idealist writings of the inter-war period with those of the 1970s, suggests that there are 'crucial differences which make the latter less easy to dismiss than the former'?[23]

None of the foregoing claims are without substance. There is no gainsaying the main thrust of points (1), (2) and (4) that there has been a considerable development of social-science techniques, that present utopian writings appear to pay self-conscious attention to 'transition strategies' and that they have generally cast their international-order net more widely to take in other issues and other values apart from those of war/peace. Nonetheless, a few qualifications are in order to place these claims in their proper perspective.

First, let us consider the question of 'methodological underpinnings'. At the most simplistic level, it might be retorted that changes in the nature of the tools employed should not deflect us from a recognition of the continuity in the basic nature of the enterprise. However, such superficial treatment might beg the very question that is being asked. In a sense, the issue here is no less than that of the status of political science versus the variants of the classical or traditional approach. The *raison d'être* of the behavioural revolution in political science was nothing if not the assertion of the claim that there is a qualitative difference in the type of 'knowledge' generated by the two methods. If this claim is allowed, then *prima facie* current utopians, by dint of the behavioural revolution itself, are *not* engaged in an age-old enterprise but in a fairly recent one. Obviously, this issue is too complex to be dealt with here and is mentioned only in passing. However, it is perhaps worth pointing out that, at least as far as those who have written under the WOMP label are concerned, their output

seems to be much more typical of classical political writing than of the new political science, not least for its ubiquitous normative flavour.

Again, it is worth examining more closely the precise nature of the claim that is being based on the sophistication of 'methodological underpinnings'. To return to Cox's three styles of future-oriented thinking, it might be argued that the full force of social-science technique has been demonstrated more in the positivist–evolutionary approach than in the natural–rational mode at present under consideration.[24] The Club of Rome's *Limits to Growth* might be taken as representative of this style of future thinking. And yet, it is evident from the controversy aroused by that study, that computerised projections of the future are, to say the least, not without their pitfalls. In other words, if we are to understand Beres and Targ to be saying that methodological sophistication provides us with scientific information about the future, then the claim, even if true in principle, has as yet not been substantiated in practice.

As regards the commitment to 'transition strategies', a useful point has been made by one of the contributors to the WOMP parent study[25] and taken up by Tom Farer in his review article. Farer writes of Mendlovitz: 'Sometimes he appears to see distinction in the project's triadic effort to link candidly preferred values to a concrete utopia through an elaborated strategy of transition. But von Weizacker is right, I believe, in seeing this as the standard form of "intellectual activism".'[26] If this is the case, then the issue of the originality of the WOMP studies resolves itself into the straightforward practical task of assessing whether (say) Falk provides his strategy of transition in more convincing detail than do earlier generations of utopians (say Sohn and Clark) when they write about their preferred international orders. Suffice it to say that it is not self-evident that such a comparison would pronounce in favour of the former.

As regards the range of goals being sought by utopians, there is a sense, of course, in which schemes for international-order reform, even the classical ones, have never been exclusively concerned to promote peace. The early European irenists were as often seeking to promote hegemonistic claims, or devising schemes to repel the infidel, as they were concerned with the

attainment of peace.[27] Furthermore, to exclude moral goals from Rousseau's and Kant's writings and to reduce them merely to projects for perpetual peace would be an act of intellectual violence. Consequently, to base the originality of the present-day utopians upon the breadth of their normative goals, is, in some respects, historically questionable. Moreover, Farer has argued cogently, even if somewhat contemptuously, that the claim to originality can scarcely rest upon the nature of the specific values that WOMP seeks to advance because, collectively, they have 'all the controversial grittiness a commitment to motherhood enjoyed in a simpler age'.[28]

The validity of point (3), the scope of the present global crisis, will be considered in due course. It has to be reserved for special mention because it relates to the main thesis of this chapter. As will be seen, whereas it is possible to assert a 'new' prospect of success for international-order reform on the basis of the nature of this crisis, it is nonetheless the specific link between crisis and reform that places current utopian thought firmly within an age-old tradition rather than marking a departure from it. Indeed, it is precisely the emphasis on crisis that makes current international-order reform part of the utopian tradition and underlines the continuities, more than the discontinuities, in this tradition.

THE KANTIAN TRADITION

For the purposes of the present discussion, it will be argued that Kant is representative of a specific form of utopian thought, and that successive waves of twentieth-century utopian writers have all been heir to this Kantian heritage. It is not intended to provide an elaborate treatment of Kant's analysis of perpetual peace, as this has been adequately done elsewhere[29] but a brief outline of his views is nonetheless necessary in order to establish his utopian 'credentials'.

The starting point of any discussion of Kant's theory of international politics would have to be his definition of the cause of the problem of war. For Kant, the basic cause of international strife is individual human nature. He speaks of 'the depravity of human nature' which 'is exhibited without disguise in the unre-

strained relations of the Nations to each other'[30] and also of war as 'requiring no special motive: . . . it appears to be ingrafted on human nature'.[31] The evil consequences of man's nature are, Kant argues, checked at the domestic level by the institution of government but, unfortunately, this only succeeds in displacing the problem:

What avails it to labour at the arrangement of a Commonwealth as a Civil Constitution regulated by law among individual men? The same unsociableness which forced men to it, becomes again the cause of each Commonwealth assuming the attitude of uncontrolled freedom in its external relations, that is, as one State in relation to other States; and consequently, any one State must expect from any other the same sort of evils as oppressed individual men and compelled them to enter into a Civil Union regulated by law.[32]

In other words, the attempt to escape anarchy at the individual level merely leads to anarchy at the level of relations between states.

Up to this point, Kant appears to be following the logic of the domestic analogy, setting the scene for an 'international' social contract. However, this is not Kant's solution. Many people wrongly believe that Kant was advocating a form of world government but this is not the case and he is quite explicit on this point. In advocating his league for peace (*foedus pacificum*) as a surrogate for a world governmental authority, Kant insists that this league 'will not aim at the acquisition of any of the political powers of a State'[33] and also that, for the league to function 'would not require these States to subject themselves . . . to public laws and to coercion under them'.[34]

There are various ways in which Kant might be characterised as a utopian. The first prerequisite of utopian thinking is, necessarily, a degree of dissatisfaction with the current order of things. Kant quite clearly feels that the state of war between nations is a morally distasteful condition and one that must be improved upon. Apart even from their moral reprehensibility, Kant viewed contemporary international politics as mechanically unsound. In his own words 'a lasting Universal Peace on the basis of the so-called Balance of Power in Europe is a mere chimera. It is like the house which was built by an architect so perfectly in accordance with all the laws of equilibrium, that when a sparrow lighted upon it, it immediately fell.'[35]

Kant's dismissal of the present is related to an optimistic faith in the future. It was argued earlier that the stamp of the utopian is his belief in progress and this is unquestionably immanent in the Kantian philosophy: 'I venture to assume that as the human race is continually advancing in civilization and culture as its natural purpose, so it is continually making progress for the better in relation to the moral end of its existence and that this progress, although it may be sometimes interrupted, will never be entirely broken off or stopped.'[36] Such progress is, in fact, guaranteed by the teleology of his philosophy, which sees mankind advancing towards some ultimate goal, and this goal is to be attained through what is basically a dialectical process between man and nature: nature imposes afflictions and hardships upon man and, in overcoming these, man is gradually guided towards his moral destiny. Progress towards perpetual peace is part of nature's grand design and is guaranteed by nature herself.

In holding this belief in progress, Kant clearly rejects a major element of 'realist' thinking, namely the view that we can project from the past into the future and that we must be guided in the future by our experience of the past. In one passage, Kant gives a powerful demonstration of his utopian bent:

This hope of better times, without which an earnest desire to do something conducive to the common well-being would never have warmed the human heart, has always exercised an influence upon the practical conduct of the well-disposed of mankind ... Arguments from experience against the success of such endeavours, resolved and carried out in hope, are of no avail. For the fact that something has not yet succeeded is no proof that it will never succeed.[37]

Kant, therefore, shares some general utopian predispositions. It remains only to discuss the particular form of his utopianism that has been his most conspicuous legacy to his successors. In its most rudimentary form, the basis of Kant's utopianism, the font of his optimism, is an argument from necessity directly to a solution – that it is necessity itself which ensures the emergence of a solution. As Kant was to express it succinctly, speaking of the adversities of war, 'the very evils which thus arise compel men to find out means against them'.[38]

This theme, that progress is created by adversity, is Kant's most distinctive refrain, as the following passages from the *Idea for a Universal History* demonstrate:

Nature has accordingly again used the unsociableness of men, and even of great societies and political bodies, her creatures of this kind, as a means to work out through their mutual antagonism a condition of rest and security. She works through wars, through the strain of never relaxed preparation for them and through the necessity which every state is at last compelled to feel within itself, even in the midst of peace, to begin some imperfect efforts to carry out her purpose.

However visionary this idea may appear to be ... it is nevertheless the inevitable issue of the necessity in which men involve one another. For this necessity must compel the Nations to the very resolution ... to which the savage in his uncivilized state, was so unwillingly compelled ... All wars are, accordingly, so many attempts ... to bring about new relations between the Nations: and by destruction or at least dismemberment of them all to form new political corporations.

By the expenditure of all the resources of the Commonwealth in military preparations against each other, by the devastations occasioned by war, and still more by the necessity of holding themselves continually in readiness for it, the full development of the capacities are undoubtedly retarded in their progress; but, on the other hand, the very evils which thus arise, compel men to find out means against them.[39]

It should also be pointed out that, even if nowhere explicitly stated by Kant, it is at least implicit in the logic of his argument that if necessity fathers its own solution, then by extension, an intensified necessity holds out even greater prospects for beneficial transformation. In essence, the structure of the Kantian argument is as follows: adversity forces man to overcome it; the greater the adversity – the more pressing the need to resolve a problem – the greater the expectation that men will behave rationally and take the appropriate steps towards meeting the emergency.

THE TWENTIETH-CENTURY 'NEO-KANTIANS'

It is this optimistic Kantian paradox that good will come out of adversity that best characterises twentieth-century thought about international-order reform. That this is so, and that the argument rests upon an apparent paradox, has been attested to by several analysts. Niebuhr for instance, has criticised latter-day utopians on the grounds that 'virtually all arguments for world government rest upon the simple presupposition that the desirability of

world order proves the attainability of world government'.[40] Likewise, Louis Beres provides a perfect example of Kantian reasoning in the context of current utopian prognoses. He argues that the success of current forms of internationalism 'is apt to depend significantly upon the perceived urgency of the developing planetary crisis' and then proceeds to highlight

the seemingly contradictory argument that the appearance of a most desirable system of world order would require an increasing proximity to a most undesirable one. Doesn't this demonstrate a strikingly illogical . . . sort of reasoning? After all, can it be argued plausibly that to improve the world we must first bring it even closer to the very configurations of global calamity we seek to avert?[41]

This neatly places current utopians within the Kantian tradition. However, to broaden out the argument, it may be contended that all three successive waves of twentieth-century utopian writing have conformed to the Kantian mould. These three successive waves that can be distinguished are: the post-1914 generation of utopians; the utopian reaction to the nuclear revolution; and, thirdly, the utopian reaction, of the 1970s, to a perceived 'planetary' crisis.[42] The pervasive influence of Kantian reasoning in each of these phases can be amply demonstrated.

As regards the post-1914 utopians, it can be argued that the case for the League of Nations was based on no more certain foundation than the necessity of avoiding a repetition of the disaster of the 1914–18 war. The optimism that the League could, in fact, induce a change for the better in standards of international behaviour was explicitly connected with the magnitude of destruction in the First World War, which convinced some utopians that it was a disaster of the necessary Kantian proportions to evince fundamental change in human conduct. Nowhere was this kind of logic employed more clearly than in the utterances of Woodrow Wilson himself who argued directly from necessity to success when he stated of the League that 'if it won't work, it must be made to work'.[43] The structure of this argument has been nicely summarised by E. H. Carr:

The advocate of a scheme for an international police force or for 'collective security' or for some other project for an international order generally replied to the criticism not by an argument designed to show how and why he thought his plan will work but by a statement that it

must be made to work because the consequences of its failure to work would be so disastrous.[44]

The utopian prescriptions of the post-1945 period, and especially those centred upon the impact of nuclear weapons, fall into precisely the same pattern of thought. These writings are too diverse to be considered in any detail but the general tenor of their conclusions make them a part of the neo-Kantian tradition. In fact, the Kantian connection is explicitly made in the title of one such book *Annihilation and Utopia*, which directly associates the necessity with the solution.[45] Examples of this logical structure are profuse. Writing in the late 1940s, R. M. Hutchins expounded his faith in world government in the following terms:

> Before the atomic bomb, we could take world government or leave it. We could rely on the long process of evolution to bring world community and world government hand in hand. Any such program today means another war, and another war means the end of civilization. *The slogan of our faith today must be, world government is necessary and therefore possible.*[46]

That this is the principal theme of post-nuclear-weapon utopian writing has been averred by Richard Falk who observes that 'after the atomic explosions at Hiroshima and Nagasaki in World War II, the plea of world order reformers has rested on a claim of alleged necessity. In other words, the argument for reform is backed up by an assertion that the existing system is heading for destruction.'[47]

Perhaps the most sophisticated and the most erudite exposition of this line of reasoning is to be found in the writing of Karl Jaspers who considers the view that 'total peril engenders total deliverance. An extreme emergency compels forms of political existence which make not only the bomb but war itself impossible.'[48] Extremity alone can produce the required transformation of people's consciousness and consequently Jaspers concludes that 'what needs increasing is the fear of the people: this should grow to overpowering force, not of blind submissiveness, but of a bright, transforming ethos that will bring forth appropriate statesmen and support their actions'.[49] It is a logic that Niebuhr could not share: 'Undoubtedly fear may be a creative force ... But the creative power of fear does not increase in proportion to its intensity.'[50] However, even in the act of denying

its logic, Niebuhr further affirms the almost universal attraction of post-1945 utopians to the Kantian model.

The third wave of twentieth-century utopian writing is that centred upon fears of some form of ecological or planetary crisis – what we might loosely term the doomsday syndrome. It is not intended to create the impression that all discussions of the perceived 'global crisis' end on a note of strident optimism that declares the emergency will be met but, at the very least, it would be difficult to deny the existence of a widespread sentiment that this 'crisis' has, at last, made the earth ripe for world-order reform.[51] It is certainly this connection which Barbara Ward sought to establish in her popularisation of the concept of 'Space Ship Earth', and it has become virtually a hypnotic chant in the writings of the 1970s. Wagar, within earshot of the 'Crack of Doom', has issued his injunction that 'we must totalise the search for world order. We must become architects and builders of civilization. Anything less is too little.'[52] Camilleri echoes the cry: 'The very magnitude of the twentieth century crisis and the structural disorder from which it springs have reinforced the natural predisposition of utopian thinking towards a revolutionary conception of change.'[53] The literature, in finest Kantian style, is replete with 'necessities' and 'imperatives'. As G. Hirschfield has expressed it: 'in no century before ours has the need for human unity been so imperative. Indeed, mankind is already unified in a material sense. It is this very fact that renders higher orders of synthesis necessary, if mankind is to survive.[54] However, probably no one has sounded the Kantian apocalyptic note more effectively than Richard Falk himself:

It is possible that the credible threat of catastrophe will generate the will and energy to overcome some bad features of our human existence that we have taken for granted or accepted as unavoidable. I would argue, in fact, that the precariousness of human survival might at last give mankind the opportunity to create a social, economic and political order that would allow human groups to live together under conditions of mutual respect and tolerable dignity.[55]

Falk, be it noted, is not always so optimistic and despite his powerful utopianism, has occasionally shed his Kantian mantle. In one passage, he indeed strikes at the very heart of the Kantian position when he solemnly counsels that 'declarations of ecologi-

cal emergency' have, in themselves, 'no capacity to induce fundamental world order reform' or, at least, not in a 'progressive' direction.[56] On balance, however, he seems more predisposed towards the alternative view. In fact, the very purpose of his book rests on the contrary assumption that such declarations of emergency can play a positive role in world-order reform.

'NECESSITY' AND 'EXTREMITY'

Before I continue with the assessment of current utopian thought, it may be useful if I examine in slightly more detail two of the key elements in the structure of these arguments, namely that of necessity and that of extremity or disaster. Philosophically, the concept of necessity, on its own, is virtually meaningless when applied to human affairs unless supported by some more general ideological or philosophical position. In fact, as with Rapoport's discussion of 'probability',[57] we might distinguish two usages of the term 'necessity'. In the first sense, necessity resides 'in the events' themselves; in the second, necessity represents a 'degree of belief' on the part of the analyst or human participant. Rapoport explains the two senses of the word 'probability' in the following terms. Probability resides 'in the events' when we can point to an observed frequency of the occurrence of a particular event (e.g. a 50% probability that a coin will come down heads). This is so because, other things being equal, we could in principle, explain this occurrence in terms of some general scientific law or laws. Rapoport contrasts this usage with the case of the 'probability of the outbreak of a nuclear war', which he denotes as representing a 'degree of belief' since 'the probability of an event such as the outbreak of a nuclear war can have nothing to do with the frequency of such events'. Rapoport then goes on to argue that 'there is a sharp distinction between this personal (or subjective) definition of probability and the definition in terms of frequencies of event'.[58] The distinction is as follows:

Implied in this degree of belief is the circumstance that the probability of an event changes in the light of what we know. Therefore, at least this kind of probability cannot reside 'in the event' if we suppose that what we know about events does not influence the events. In other words, the

something that we call the probability of an event is not ... an objective property of the event but depends on the way that we define the context in which the event is to be considered.[59]

Rapoport concludes, on the basis of the arbitrary components that enter into all calculations of probability, defined as degree of belief, that 'probabilities which we assign to events become reflections of our preferences rather than of our knowledge'.[60]

The concept of necessity can be subjected to a similar analysis. The value of doing this is that it helps us to clarify precisely what the utopian argument 'from necessity' amounts to and it can be said that whereas most utopians would like to pretend that necessity is of Rapoport's first kind, 'in the events themselves', quite clearly the necessity to which they make appeal is of the second order and represents no more than a 'degree of belief'.

The only necessity that can reside in the events themselves is that of a relationship explained by some universal law. This is logically so because necessity is no more than an extreme form of 'probability' in the sense of an absolute observed frequency or 'constant conjunction'. When we depart from this usage, necessity denotes a degree of belief on the part of the observer and in this sense, to echo Rapoport, becomes 'a reflection of our preferences rather than of our knowledge'. To put this in a slightly different form, we can translate a statement about necessity in human affairs to be no more than a shorthand form of expression in which a conditional clause is suppressed. For instance, a declaration that 'world government is necessary' can be translated to mean that world government should be sought *if* certain undesirable situations are to be avoided. In other words, utopian arguments from necessity are no more than hypothetical imperatives unless they are linked to a philosophy of history that can restore the necessity to the events themselves, as Kant himself does through his conception of nature's teleological design.

Most utopian writers are, of course, painfully aware of this conventional philosophical distinction. The point, for them, then becomes, whether the latter conception of necessity can be made to approximate the former and yield a solution by means of engaging in a political process. Hence the widespread emphasis within utopian writings upon 'consciousness-raising' and Mendlovitz's candid admission, with regard to WOMP, that its

foundation was a 'conscious political act, based on a theory of social change'.[61]

The other prop of the neo-Kantian argument that deserves some attention is the idea of extremity or disaster. The role of extremity or disaster has, as was noted above, been a pervasive theme of all utopian writing on world-order reform. It should, however, be pointed out that utopians have been concerned with disaster from two distinct perspectives, both from a retrospective and from a prospective viewpoint. Indeed, it might be contended that in the past century, one of the more noticeable trends in utopian thought has been the shift of emphasis from the former to the latter as a result of which utopian arguments 'from necessity' have tended to focus upon 'previsioned' disasters rather than upon disasters already experienced.

It is an oft-repeated maxim that peace projects and world-order reform proposals have tended to crop up in the immediate aftermath of calamitous wars. As William Penn was to express it in his *Essay on Peace* (1693), mankind cannot 'finally know the comfort of peace but by the smart and penance of the vices of war'.[62] However the 'smart and penance' of war can make its influence felt in two ways, either by direct experience or by an act of creative imagination projected towards the future. It is interesting, therefore, to note Hinsley's observation that 'it was in the last years of the nineteenth century that for the first time in the history of the present European based world civilisation . . . peace proposals were propagated for fear of the danger of war rather than in consequence of its outbreak'.[63] If Hinsley is correct, then we might optimistically judge that there is a learning process at work here. The neo-Kantian argument from future necessities is very similar to the argument from past disasters in the sense that the 'heightened danger' thesis is logically similar to retrospective explanations of interest in peace projects in the aftermath of major wars. The central concept is still that of extremity: what changes is merely our chronological relationship to it. Indeed, it might be contended that this has been the major purpose of recent utopian thought – to make 'anticipated disasters' serve as functional substitutes for 'actual disasters' and so derive the benefits of disasters before they occur. If this can be achieved, it might be taken as a sign of progress. It

is for this reason that Jaspers, as was noted above, placed great weight on the creative role of fear – the previsioned dread of nuclear war. If disaster can produce a cathartic effect, it is as well to utilise the threat of it as the actual experience of it. This was certainly Kant's preference: 'And, at last, after many devastations, overthrows, and even complete internal exhaustion of their powers, the nations are driven forward to the goal *which Reason might have well impressed upon them, even without so much sad experience.*'[64]

Returning to the issue of the novelty, or otherwise, of the current utopian position, there would seem to be two other aspects of the question worthy of consideration. The argument thus far has established that most current utopian writing falls within the neo-Kantian tradition because of its emphasis on 'solutions' generated by 'necessity'. Even within this tradition, however, it could be argued that present-day utopian prescriptions differ from those of the past as a result of the specific nature of the threat that they consider is presented to the global order. This argument has at least two strands to it. The first would have it that current global necessities are more likely to issue in international-order reform than previously because of the *source* of the threat to the system. The second maintains that the present crisis will issue in reform because of its specific quality of *terminality*. These arguments will be considered in turn.

Classical 'social contract' or 'domestic analogy' prescriptions for the ills of international anarchy and for overcoming the traditional dilemmas of national military security have always suffered from an inherent tension: that it is with those very states that constitute the source of the threat that co-operation must be entered into in order to eliminate the threat. As Hedley Bull has remarked in connection with this central paradox of the social-contract school:

The idea of world government by contract involves a dilemma ... if states are indeed in a Hobbesian state of nature, the contract by means of which they are to emerge from it cannot take place ... The difficulty ... is that the description it contains of the actual condition of international relations, and the prescription it provides for its improvement, are inconsistent with one another.[65]

That is to say that the very nature of the issue of military security, because of its inherent zero-sum nature, makes 'trust'

between the contracting parties difficult and renders the basis of co-operation tenuous. No utopian prescription has been able to rise above this military security dilemma and this, most analysts would agree, lies at the heart of the repeated historical failures to institute some form of collective security system.

However, it soon becomes apparent that those utopians currently arguing from the basis of a more wide-ranging 'planetary security dilemma' regard this as constituting a major watershed in utopian writing and see it as providing an enhanced prospect for world-order reform. The thrust of the argument here is that the contemporary crisis is not one that has its source in a *competitive game between states* but rather one that has its source in a *co-operative game against Nature*. Thus, according to its proponents, the planetary crisis marks a breach with traditional utopian concerns because the danger is located in a different source – nature itself – and this novel dimension to the problem, while bringing with it the prospect of ultimate catastrophe, brings with it also a greater prospect of achieving the reform necessary to avert that disaster. The argument remains within the Kantian mould but not so much on the basis of the extremity of the crisis as on the basis of its source.

That the global environmental crisis is qualitatively different in nature from traditional military security concerns and that there is for that very reason a heightened possibility of its leading to co-operative and constructive international-order reform are propositions that have found widespread recent support. They underlie virtually all utopian writing of the 1970s. The view is perhaps most succinctly expressed in the following quotation from a recent article: 'The traditional concern of functionalists and others interested in world order systems has been the elimination of war and in this context nationalism has been understandably viewed as a major obstacle. However, when the focus shifts to confronting the environmental crisis national egoism assumes a less threatening dimension.'[66] The same authors explain their reasoning in greater detail, emphasising the inherent difference between 'environmental' security and 'military' security and underlining the co-operation-inducing nature of the former as compared with the co-operation-inhibiting nature of the latter:

there is the amorphous and unplanned accumulation of environmental stress, especially in the form of pollution and population growth. While engendering definite destabilising consequences, their root causes are not traceable to specific conflict producing intent on the part of any one country ... Any initiative for cooperation, however, will come primarily from the realization on the part of individual states of the extent to which their security is threatened in the absence of cooperation.[67]

Even such a renowned 'realist' as George Kennan has given expression to the same kind of sentiment, albeit in a less grandiose form, when he argued that co-operation on environmental matters might 'spill over' into, and thereby improve, the international atmosphere generally.[68]

The argument is not as compelling as its seductive simplicity would suggest. As has been argued above, traditionally, supranational solutions have been unattractive because they have required co-operation amongst competitive consumers of security. Is this difficulty overcome by the 'external'-threat imagery of an increasingly malevolent nature? Ostensibly, as Shields and Ott have argued, it should make a difference. However, a moment's reflection suggests that there is no very convincing reason why this should be so. To the extent that the prevailing philosophy of war in the twentieth century has moved away from the Clausewitzian to embrace cataclysmic conceptions, especially under nuclear conditions, it can be argued that war itself (which, in these terms, no one 'wants') has constituted an exogenous threat to the system, equivalent to that of nature, without this leading to international-order reform. Moreover, it is a deceptive imagery to pretend that the 'environmental crisis' is something 'out there' which threatens us all. The environmental or planetary situation is as much a product of state policies as is the danger of war. These considerations indicate that the facile distinction between a 'state-engendered' (security) crisis and a 'nature-imposed' (environmental) crisis is simply not tenable. The recent response of states to the 'endangered planet' image serves to reinforce this conclusion: if the environmental degradation and 'limit to growth' arguments have had any concrete impact on international politics, then it has surely been to cast states in the roles of competitive consumers of utiles, be they military or welfare/environmental, and, if anything, to intensify

the zero-sum nature of *all* international political games, including those of growth and development, as well as the traditional ones of military security.

The last aspect to be considered is whether there is a new force to utopian arguments from necessity because of the 'terminality' of the conditions facing mankind. There is undoubtedly a widespread feeling that this is so – that even if the prospect of disaster has not induced reform in the past, this was because the disaster would be only partial and temporary whereas any future disaster will be total and permanent. The Kantian logic here is that even if the international body politic has not been moved to reform by periodic bouts of influenza, it must nonetheless activate itself when confronted with imminent terminal cancer.

The issue, as posed, is not open to answer. If we recall the previous discussion of the concept of necessity, there seems no sound 'logical' reason why a terminal crisis should possess a greater reform-producing capacity than any other crisis, except in so far as (and this may be a major qualification) the terminality is recognised and acted upon as such. Perception and understanding are, of course, the mainsprings of human action and there is some reason for believing that humans are impressed by the notion of terminality. A good example can be offered from a different, but related, context. In the course of a discussion of Herman Kahn's ideas on nuclear war, Anatole Rapoport makes the following observation:

> Kahn categorically rejects both the idea that the prospect of the horrors of nuclear war has made it 'unthinkable' and the idea that if such a war occurs it will be the 'end of civilization' ... I believe that the choice of the notation (World War IV, World War V) was meant to dissociate 'World War III' from 'finality'.[69]

If Rapoport's interpretation of Kahn's motivations is substantially correct, as I believe it is, one wonders why Kahn should have been perturbed by any glimmer of 'finality'. The apparent explanation must be that Kahn was writing a tract about the continuing utility of the Clausewitzian war-system and, as such, was seeking to counteract 'revolutionary' thinking about nuclear warfare: one can, therefore, only suppose that Kahn was afraid that talk of 'finality' would lead to pusillanimous thinking and, perhaps, induce that very reform of the war-system which Kahn was seeking to prevent.

If we allow this argument, it may be the case that the 'terminality' of the heralded world-order crisis represents a watershed in utopian thought. At the very least, there is reason for suspecting that on the basis of this perceived terminal condition, there has been some reversion, to use Mannheim's terms, from the 'liberal–humanitarian' tradition of utopian thought to an earlier 'chiliastic' tradition.[70] Mannheim distinguishes them as follows:

> The fulfilment of chiliast expectations may occur at any moment. Now with the liberal–humanitarian idea the utopian element received a definite location in the historical process – it is the culmination point of historical evolution. In contrast with the earlier conception of a utopia which was suddenly to break upon the world completely from the outside, this signifies, in the long run, a relative toning down of the notion of sudden historical change.[71]

In these terms the utopian writings of the 1970s have much in common with the chiliastic tradition.

It has been the argument of this chapter that twentieth-century utopian writings, despite some differences of approach and emphasis, fall overwhelmingly within a broader utopian tradition that may be labelled the neo-Kantian. If we have presently arrived at a watershed in utopian thought, and this is by no means clear, then the most convincing grounds for asserting such a claim seem to derive from the nature of the present 'crisis' that is 'necessitating' reform and especially from its avowed 'terminality'.

In a sense, therefore, the uniqueness of present utopian writings hinges upon the objective existence of this crisis itself – on whether it is as threatening as its utopian analysts claim it to be. If the doomsday prognosis is correct, the perceived necessity becomes more compelling than ever before. If the crisis of today is no more pressing and no more terminal than those of yore, historians may well look back upon the utopianism of Richard Falk, in two centuries' time, with the same indulgence that we can now look back upon the utopianism of Kant.

In the final analysis, we are back to 'degrees of belief'. As Jaspers has observed 'despair and confidence are moods not insights'.[72] If there is anything distinctive about the current *genre* of international-order writing, it is its sense of urgency. This sentiment may be soundly based; alternatively, it may be no

more than a demonstration of the egocentricity of an age that chooses to believe its crises are the culmination or *dénouement* of history – a mood, as commentators have noted, that is especially prone to strike as we approach the *fin de millennium*. What we do not yet know is whether this utopian mood is also an insight.

3   Rousseau and the tradition of despair

This chapter will be similar in structure to the previous one: it will consist of an outline of the general traits of the realist interpretation of international politics, will demonstrate the development of the attitude of despair within the writings of Jean-Jacques Rousseau, will seek to show how this attitude has been bequeathed to, and elaborated upon by, twentieth-century realists and, finally, will discuss in greater detail some of the key elements embraced within this philosophical perspective. As in the previous chapter, the main concentration will be upon continuities within this particular tradition of thought.

There is, of course, a degree of artificiality in speaking of realist or utopian schools or traditions of thought as, indeed, there is in assuming that we can readily discern a sharp dichotomy between the two. Frequently, writers display 'hybrid' characteristics, which makes it difficult, not to say unproductive, to try to insert them into convenient 'realist' or 'utopian' pigeon-holes. Nonetheless, as long as it is remembered that we are talking at the level of intellectual ideal-types, there is some value in depicting the general characteristics of a realist tradition of thought. As Brian Porter has observed, '"the tradition" then is a device, as the arranging of stars in constellations is a device, for the convenience of the observer ... "Permanent propensities of the political mind" might be a better, though more cumbersome, way of putting it.'[1]

What are the dominant features of a realist understanding of international politics? Most obviously, realism is associated with the fearsome and depressing world of power politics in which states have to be permanently on their guard if life is not to be 'nasty, brutish and short'. It is associated with the imagery of the state as a gladiator engaged in a perpetual combat. As one writer has summarised it, realism entails 'being aware of the grim necessities of communal existence and (of) being able to see that man is prone to fight, to seek power and to pursue his own egotistical ends. Its basic premise is that international relations

are anarchic and lawless, and its basic proposition is that all states seek to enhance their own power.'[2]

According to Waltz, an exhaustive listing of the elements of a *Realpolitik* approach would be as follows:

The ruler's, and later the state's interest provides the spring of action; the necessities of policy arise from the unregulated competition of states; political calculation based on these necessities can discover rational policies; success is the ultimate test of policy, and success is defined as preserving and strengthening the state. Ever since Machiavelli, interest and necessity – and *raison d'état* the phrase that comprehends them – have remained the key concepts of Realpolitik.[3]

It can be seen from this quotation that the idea of necessity is as prominent in the realist tradition as it was in the Kantian utopian one but with quite different implications – a point that will be discussed later in the chapter.

More specifically, it can be contended that realist thought is a composite of some six different aspects: some of these, as is to be expected, will simply be the obverse of elements of utopianism considered in the foregoing chapter.

In the first place, it has been argued that one of the main characteristics of utopianism was its belief in the attainability of progress in terms of the realisation of a preferable international order. Utopianism is nothing if not a reformist attitude of mind. What is important for our present study is the fact that realism, as a pessimistic tradition, denies the possibility of progress. For the realist, power politics is the name of the game, always has been and always will be. Accordingly, the parameters of realist thought are set by the boundaries of historical experience and the propositions derived from it depend 'for their validity mainly on historical precedent in the field of state practice'.[4]

As opposed to the linear conception of historical development posited in utopian thinking, the realist conception is a cyclical one. In the words of Hedley Bull,

As against the belief of the 'idealists' in progress they drew attention to the cyclical or recurrent patterns of international politics. Contrary to the view of the 'idealists' that power politics was a method of conducting international relations that belonged only to the bad old world, they presented power politics as the law of all international life.[5]

Similarly, Nicholas Spykman had written in 1942 that 'the new order will not differ from the old, and international society will

continue to operate with the same fundamental power patterns. It will be a world of power politics' and that 'there seems to be no reason to assume or expect that these behaviour patterns of states will suddenly change or disappear'.[6]

This feature of international politics is permanent and since states and statesmen cannot rise above it, there can, therefore, be no significant progress in international life. However, the reasons offered by realists for the non-attainability of progress differ from writer to writer. For some, the belief that wars and violence will always be a feature of international life is grounded upon a theory of human nature – a theory that regards this nature as base, wicked and unchangeable. Since the raw material of politics, namely people themselves, is unchanging, there can be no amelioration of the kind of political order that they produce.

Other realists do not have, or do not emphasise, such a gloomy appreciation of human nature. For them, the permanence of the worst features of international political life derives, not from human nature, but from the systemic setting in which states find themselves. As John Herz, the foremost theorist of the 'security dilemma' has noted, 'realist thought is determined by an insight into the overpowering impact of the security factor and the ensuing power-political, oligarchic, authoritarian and similar trends and tendencies in society and politics'.[7] This security dilemma Herz has outlined in the following terms, as a product of the anarchic setting of states:

Groups or individuals living in such a constellation must be, and usually are, concerned about their security from being attacked, subjected, dominated, or annihilated by other groups and individuals. Striving to attain security from such attack, they are driven to acquire more and more power in order to escape the impact of the power of others. This, in turn, renders the others more insecure and compels them to prepare for the worst. Since none can ever feel entirely secure in such a world of competing units, power competition ensues, and the vicious circle of security and power accumulation is on.[8]

As there is no way of breaking out of this circle, the power political aspects of international life are repetitive and unchanging and attempts to 'perfect' the system are doomed to failure.

Secondly, by comparison with utopians, realists hold a more deterministic view of the historical process and allow correspond-

ingly less scope for the intervention of human agency in the design and implementation of international order. Such order as there is, is in a sense already immanent within the historical process and cannot be grafted onto the system artificially from the outside. As was argued earlier, realists tend to see the historical process driven along by antecedent causes rather than by conscious human design. To that extent, we may seek to understand the process of historical change but not to control it: people tend to be the objects of history, not its subjects.

From this perspective, it is worth pointing out that political realism has undergone a curious metamorphosis and has ended up with a nuance which was originally quite alien to it. In its original formulation, the one we tend to associate with the name of Machiavelli, the principles of realism underwrote a political programme that was at once active, interventionist and predicated upon the assumption that much could be achieved by conscious political design and artifact. Although we recognise Machiavelli as the founding father of *Realpolitik*, it is one of the ironies of history that his prince would have to be regarded as the quintessential utopian, the man with the political vision and the *virtū* necessary to implement it. Thus, in its early manifestations, with Hobbes as well as with Machiavelli, realism was to be associated with the active pursuit and creation of political order: only later, and particularly in the context of international order, was realism to emphasise the limitations upon the politician's craft. The statesman whose supreme achievement was the creation of the modern state, was to become impotent when confronted with the chaos prevailing in the global whole.

There no longer is, in Morse's phrase, 'a realist assumption of masterless man'.[9] Realism has, if you will, lost its political nerve: it has moved from a concentration upon goals to an obsession with harmful consequences. At best this leads to complacency in which realists 'succumb to the temptation which Mannheim identified as the hallmark of conservative thought: the belief in the "here and now" – that Utopia is always embedded in existing reality'.[10] At worst, it leads to the paralysis of the political spirit, demonstrated in the admonition of a man who perhaps had more spirit than most: 'men are dangerous not only because they have unlimited appetites and unlimited yearning for power, but be-

cause they are creatures with dreams; and their extravagant dreams turn into nightmares if they seek to realise them in history'.[11]

The third and fourth elements of realism may be dealt with together as they are merely negatives of points already made with reference to utopianism. These were a belief in the power of rationality and, related to this the acceptance of a universal harmony of interests. Both of these would be denied by the realist for reasons that found their classic exposition in E. H. Carr's *The Twenty Years' Crisis*. Rationality alone will be as likely to lead to conflict as to harmony because it will recognise that 'the clash of interests is real and inevitable'. Carr, therefore, urges that 'the reality of conflict be frankly recognised'. Basically, Carr's point was that there are antagonistic national interests and that attempts to assert a universal international interest *per se* are, in consequence, specious. In fact, using a variant of Marx's theory of ideology, Carr argues that all expressions of internationalism are little more than the (conscious or unconscious) rationalisation of the interests of the dominant states within international society. When utopians make appeal to universal standards of justice and claim that it is in the interests of all mankind to observe them, they are, according to Carr, appealing to spurious principles. He, therefore, attacks the residual natural-law elements in the utopian school upon which their belief in rationality and harmony is based. Carr's indictment ran as follows:

The charge is not that human beings fail to live up to their principles . . . What matters is that these supposedly absolute and universal principles were not principles at all but the unconscious reflexions of national policy based on a particular interpretation of national interest . . . The bankruptcy of utopianism resides not in its failure to live up to its principles but in the exposure of its inability to provide any absolute and disinterested standard for the conduct of international affairs.[12]

In any case, for the realist, rationality was a two-edged weapon, having within it the potential for good but without any guarantee that this was its only potential. As Niebuhr was to phrase it in his critique of the rationality inherited from the Enlightenment:

The historical development of freedom was believed to be purely creative partly because it was believed that increased freedom meant

increasing rationality; and increasing reason was tantamount to increasing disinterestedness which would overcome both injustice and par-
ochialism ... Unfortunately, the growth of freedom had more ambiguous consequences than the optimists assumed. Reason, despite every
refinement, could always become the servant of interest and passion.[13]

Similarly, in a commentary upon Niebuhr's political thought,
one writer has noted that part of his legacy was 'a philosophical
perspective that assumed the futility of appeals to a "scientific"
reason or good will in social affairs and the consequent necessity
for a tough-minded use of power in the agonising quest for
"relative" justice'.[14]

Fifthly, realism has always made a distinction between individual and state codes of morality in the sense that it does not
accept that the statesman should be constrained by everyday
ethics. The statesman is a 'trustee' of the national community
and, as such, there are special demands upon him that make the
application of normal ethical codes inappropriate. Consequently,
the conscience of the office is, for the realist, quite different from
the conscience of the man and allowance must be made accordingly. It is, after all, in this very sense that *raison d'état* can be
appealed to as a justification for otherwise unacceptable activities. It is this point that Thompson makes when he remarks
that 'assertions ... that the only morality is individual morality
have to be seen in the light of the differences between the
individual and the collectivity and the imperatives to which each
must respond'.[15]

Lastly, and perhaps most decisive of all, realists see states
locked in a situation of perpetual competition with each other for
the simple reason that they cannot generate enough trust in each
other to allow them to escape from this situation. Moreover, in
these circumstances, the statesman, according to realist precepts,
would be derelict in his duty if he acted upon trust with no
assurance of reciprocity on the part of other states. The tragic
results that flow from this absence of trust have been summarised
by Jervis: 'Because there are no institutions or authorities that
can make and enforce international laws, the policies of co-
operation that will bring mutual rewards if others co-operate
may bring disaster if they do not. Because states are aware of this,
anarchy encourages behaviour that leaves all concerned worse off

than they could be.'[16] However, nowhere has this situation been better analysed than in Meinecke's classic exposition of the doctrine of *raison d'état:*

But why is it not possible for the properly-understood interest of the States themselves, co-operating by reason of ethical motives, to induce them to unite and freely restrict the methods of their power politics, to abide by law and morality, and to develop the institution of International Law and the League of Nations to a full and satisfactory efficiency? Because no one of them will trust another round the corner. Because no one of them believes for certain about any of the others, that it would abide by the agreed limitations in absolutely every instance and without any exception; but on the contrary suspects that in certain instances that other would once again lapse into following his own natural egoism. The first lapse back into evil ways on the part of one state (out of anxiety for its own welfare) and attended by success, would be sufficient to shatter the whole undertaking once again, and destroy the credit of ethical policy. Even if one wished to conduct the foreign policy of one's own state by methods which were not ethically objectionable, one would nevertheless always have to be on one's guard in case one's opponent failed to do so too; and in such a case one would feel oneself released from the moral imperative – whereupon the old, age-old game would then start again from the beginning.[17]

ROUSSEAU AND THE TRADITION OF DESPAIR

In this section, it is proposed to do the same as was done in the discussion of Kant. Briefly, I will outline Rousseau's general discussion of international politics – his conception of the problem and its solution – and, secondly, proceed to a systematic examination of the realist elements within his philosophy. As I have previously associated Kant with a tradition of optimism, Rousseau will now be located within a general tradition of despair. In other words, Rousseau can be seen as being representative of certain features of realist thinking and it is as an illustration of these patterns of thought that he is to be discussed. As with Kant, the point is that these patterns of thought are recurrent and are as conspicuous today as they were two centuries ago.

Man, in the state of nature, is not for Rousseau a warlike creature. He is peaceful and timid, more prone to run away than to fight. Whence, then, does the violence of international politics arise? What is the source of war? War, Rousseau repeatedly

asserts, is a social phenomenon, social in the sense that what gives rise to it is the inception of civil society and the resultant nature of the international system. It is the move from the state of nature to civil society that makes man a fighter. As Rousseau puts it 'it is only when he has entered into society with other men that he decides to attack another, and he only becomes a soldier after he has become a citizen. There are no strong natural predispositions to make war.'[18]

Why does civil society bring about this change and produce a state of war? For the simple reason that while it solves one problem of order at the domestic level, it immediately creates another at the international: the institution of the state creates domestic order but initiates international anarchy. In Rousseau's words:

If the social order were really, as is pretended, the work not of passion but of reason, should we have been so slow to see that, in the shaping of it, either too much or too little, has been done for our happiness? that, each one of us being in the civil state as regards our fellow citizens, but in the state of nature as regards the rest of the world, we have taken all kinds of precautions against private wars only to kindle national wars a thousand times more terrible? and that, in joining a particular group of men, we have really declared ourselves the enemies of the whole race?[19]

It is in this context that one commentator's point is well made. When we, as we so readily do, compare international society with the state of nature, we should remember that this state of nature is, paradoxically, an artificial one. As Cornelia Navari has commented in a recent essay 'is not there something very odd about the "state of nature" which constitutes international relations – namely, the fact that it did not always exist? The fact that it was an *established* state of nature which emerged out of something that went before?'[20]

In any case, if this is how Rousseau views the problem of international politics, what is his proposed solution to it? Rousseau argues that, if there is a solution at all, then it lies in a confederation between the states. In other words, he duplicates the logic of the domestic analogy and contends that there must be a second social contract between the states that will remove them from the state of nature in which they find themselves.

Moreover, Rousseau pursues the logic of the domestic analogy to its fullest conclusion in the sense that, if international anarchy

is to be overcome, it must be through a confederation 'with teeth'. What Rousseau had in mind was a very strong form of supra-national organisation. Unlike the Kantian proposal, Rousseau's confederation was to have the power of enforcement and there was to be no right of secession from it. Thus whereas Kant argued that the state should not be subject to law, Rousseau insistently argued the opposite case: 'If there is any way of reconciling these dangerous contradictions, it is to be found only in such a form of federal government as shall unite nations by bonds similar to those which already unite their individual members and place the one no less than the other under the authority of the law.'[21]

Rousseau was arguing that if there was a solution, then such a federation was it. But, of course, he rejects this as a solution on the grounds that there is absolutely no hope of its realisation. As he puts it ironically, all that is needed to establish the federation is the consent of the princes who, unfortunately, 'would resist with all their might any proposal for its creation'. And so, having claimed that there is only one possible solution to the ills of international disorder, Rousseau then goes on to dismiss it as being utterly unattainable.

It is now time to consider the realist elements displayed by Rousseau's assessment of the nature and limitations of international political life. From this perspective, there are six points that have to be made.

First, Rousseau provides, in most poignant fashion, an example of the conviction that the universe is irredeemably irrational. In setting out the case for the creation of his federation, Rousseau insists that it is logically irrefutable. He is at pains to show how the individual princes, as well as international society as a whole, would benefit from such a scheme. In fact, in terms of a rational pursuit of self-interest, Rousseau is convinced that the federation has everything to commend it. Why, then, will the princes never consent to it? At the heart of Rousseau's pessimism is his conviction that men will not act rationally – that even if they are shown where their own best interests lie, they will not behave accordingly. To make this point, Rousseau introduces his distinction between 'real' and 'apparent' interests and believes that states will always pursue their apparent (short-term, selfish)

interests at the expense of their real (long-term, enlightened) interests. At the end of his section on the 'logic' of the federation, he concedes that 'this is not, of course, to say that the Sovereigns will adopt this project . . . but only that they would adopt it, if they took counsel of their true interest'.[22] Rousseau plainly suggests that they will not. If any more proof is needed for the contention that he despairs about the rationality of man and the universe, we need only recall his most famous line: 'If, in spite of all this, the project remains unrealised, that is not because it is utopian; it is because men are crazy, and because to be sane in a world of madmen is in itself a kind of madness.'[23] The quotation is significant for two reasons, not only because it reflects Rousseau's despair about human rationality, but also because it is an excellent illustration of his 'realistic' awareness of the role of trust in international affairs.

This leads us on to the second point. To be alone in pursuing 'rational' policies, when other states are not, is a form of madness because, unless you can trust the rest, then you will be the one to lose out. Standard game-theory situations, such as Prisoner's Dilemma, demonstrate this theme. The point Rousseau is making then is that if the other players are 'mad', you cannot trust their rationality or good faith and, consequently, the only 'sane' course is to act as madly as the others. From a realist point of view, Rousseau's comment is perceptive and shrewd. (Example: a sane leader in a nuclear world populated by mad national leaders would be a handicap as he could be deterred much more readily than he himself could deter.)

If realist thought centres upon this lack of trust and the consequent security dilemmas, Rousseau is an admirable exponent of this turn of mind: 'It is quite true that it would be much better for all men to remain always at peace. But so long as there is no security for this, everyone, having no guarantee that he can avoid war, is anxious to begin it at the moment which suits his own interest.'[24] He elaborates on this theme, returning to his point about sane men in a mad world: 'However salutary it may be in theory to obey the dictates of public spirit, it is certain that, politically and even morally, those dictates are liable to prove fatal to the man who persists in observing them with all the world when no one thinks of observing them towards him.'[25] As with all realist reasoning of this nature, while it is sound advice to

give to one state, it backfires when every state acts in accordance with it because the entire system becomes a vicious self-perpetuating circle.

To take Rousseau's despair one stage further on this matter: it has been an important article of faith in many of the liberal – utopian – internationalist schools of thought that growing inter-dependence and knowledge of each other's societies might help to create the basis of trust and understanding between countries, which could, in turn, elevate standards of international diplomacy. Rousseau refutes this line of argument altogether and asserts that interdependence produces conflict and not harmony. As Stanley Hoffmann has written, it is 'one of Rousseau's deepest insights, one that shatters a large part of the liberal vision of world affairs ... (that) interdependence breeds not accommodation and harmony but suspicion and incompatibility'.[26]

Thirdly, it is implicit in most of Rousseau's reasoning that he rejects that strand of utopian thought that sees the perfection of the internal constitutions of states as a path to an improved world order. Whether in its Kantian or Wilsonian formulation, Rousseau rejects this argument because war, we have seen, flows from the nature of the system irrespective of the merits or defects of the individual states. Unlike the drafters of the League of Nations, therefore, Rousseau considers that 'it is not impossible that a Republic, though in itself well-governed, should enter upon an unjust war'.[27]

Fourthly, like all realists, Rousseau perceives within the system an inherent propensity to pursue power. He paints a picture of states, obsessed by power considerations, restlessly striving to improve their relative positions. Accordingly, the pursuit of power is the central dynamic of the international system because the state 'feels weak so long as there are others stronger than itself. Its safety and preservation demand that it makes itself stronger than its neighbours. It cannot increase, foster or exercise its strength except at their expense.'[28]

Fifthly, in his attitude towards international law and towards universal peace· principles, Rousseau is the realist without peer. Everything he has said thus far conveys the conviction that states cannot be trusted and that covenants without the sword are but words. This attitude extends to his analysis of international law

and universal professions of faith in peace. In fact, on these issues, Rousseau provides a critique that is almost identical to that later developed by E. H. Carr. He dismisses international law on the very same grounds as did Carr: 'As for what is commonly called international law, because its laws lack any sanction, they are unquestionably mere illusions ... the decisions of international law, having no other guarantee than their usefulness to the person who submits to them, are only respected in so far as interest accords with them.'[29] Likewise, in reply to universalist peace sentiments, Rousseau provides the classic realist retort that 'to prove that peace, as a general principle, is a better thing than war is to say nothing to the man who has private reasons for preferring war to peace'.[30]

The sixth point takes us to the essence of Rousseau's despair, the font of his realism. As we have seen, he regards the problems of international life as being inherently insoluble, as a federation will never be adopted. On this basis he may be advanced as an exponent of the philosophy of despair as regards international politics. Probably other words would suffice just as well as 'despair' – a random selection of epithets used by commentators to describe his international political theory includes 'pessimistic', 'hopeless', 'fatalistic', 'gloomy', 'depressing', 'dismal' and 'frightening'. However, despair seems to capture the essentials of Rousseau's moral anguish at the continuance of a state of affairs that he regarded as a moral scandal. It may be objected, and a case could be made out along these lines, that there is very much of the utopian in Rousseau as well – that it is misleading to regard him as an unmitigated realist. Indeed, it could be claimed that while in his 'head' Rousseau is a realist, in his 'heart' he is a utopian. A perfect illustration of this dualism within Rousseau can be found in his Abstract of Saint-Pierre's Project. Rousseau opens in convincing utopian style:

Never did the mind of man conceive a scheme nobler, more beautiful, or more useful than that of a lasting peace between all the peoples of Europe. Never did a writer better deserve a respectful hearing than he who suggests means for putting that scheme into practice. What man, if he has a spark of goodness, but must feel his heart glow within him at so fair a prospect? Who would not prefer the illusions of a generous spirit, which overleaps all obstacles, to that dry, repulsive reason whose indifference to the welfare of mankind is ever the chief obstacle to all schemes for its attainment?[31]

Having given vent to this utopian outburst, Rousseau's realist *alter ego* quickly reasserts itself:

In these opening words, I could not refrain from giving way to the feelings which filled my heart. Now let us do our best to reason coolly.[32]

Surely this reveals both the utopian and the realist elements within Rousseau? We can sympathise with the argument but must finally reject it. The reason for doing so is as follows. If there is to be any distinction between realist and utopian philosophies, it must be on the basis of their views, not about the desirability of international-order reform, but about its attainability. Rousseau's sentiments predispose him to think such reform desirable but he holds out not a shred of hope that it can be attained. This, in itself, suffices to make Rousseau wear the realist mantle.

ROUSSEAU AND TWENTIETH-CENTURY REALISM

Rousseau's brand of realism, just like Kant's utopianism, has found fertile ground for growth in twentieth-century conditions, to such an extent that one analyst has pronounced that 'today's revolutionary system of international politics confirms the sharp and gloomy analysis of Rousseau, whose pessimism was all too easily discounted in the moderate system which died at Sarajevo'.[33]

Of the many aspects of twentieth-century realist thought, three in particular stand out as being part of the tradition of despair bequeathed by Rousseau. The first, above all, bears the imprint of Rousseau's pessimism. It emphasises the unattainability of radical change within the international order and in doing so it goes beyond Rousseau to disparage the very nature of the utopian enterprise and to warn against its inherent dangers. A reading of virtually any twentieth-century exponent of realism would reveal this constant refrain. It constitutes, for example, the very first of Morgenthau's principles of political realism in which he propounds the philosophy that 'politics ... is governed by objective laws' and that 'the operation of these laws being impervious to our preferences, men will challenge them only at the risk of failure'.[34] Later Morgenthau makes it clear that challenging the laws of power risks not only failure but indeed regression: 'How often have statesmen been motivated by the desire to improve the world, and ended by making it worse?'[35]

This theme, that the attempt consciously to initiate international order will prove to be destructive, constantly recurs in realist writings, especially from the 1930s onwards. One of its earliest proponents was later to write in this vein when he warned that 'the radical sense of the ultimate, which places the status quo of any community under the judgement of an ultimate justice, may be as dangerous as it can be creative'.[36] Likewise, Henry Kissinger, as theorist, has often-times given lugubrious warning of the hazards in pursuing radical changes to the existing order. He assures us that 'the translation into political terms of prophetic visions always falsifies the intentions of their proponents'[37] and is particularly fond of the irony inherent in the fact that 'When you know history, how many tragedies have been touched off by good will, you have to admit the tragic elements of existence.'[38]

The second element prevalent in twentieth-century realist thought might be captured in the dictum *si vis pacem para bellum*. This, in itself, is an invocation of Rousseau's logic and gives expression to the idea that in a world populated by 'madmen', it is rational to strive for peace by preparing for war: indeed, this becomes the only 'sane' policy available to national societies.

Implicit in this formulation is the assumption that in an imperfect, and imperfectible, world, the most that can be achieved is a form of 'negative' order, one in which the worst abuses of power are guarded against. The system, however, cannot move beyond this to the attainment of 'positive' order. The realist doctrine of order is 'negative' in the following sense, clearly revealed in Kissinger's definition of diplomacy as 'the art of restraining the exercise of power'.[39] It sees order as a situation of collective checkmate in which no member of the system is in a position to do damage to the others. Peace is equivalent to equilibrium and it is in the maintenance of this equilibrium, if need be by preparing for war, that peace is secured. Such is the minimum, but also the maximum, programme for the practising statesman. As has been said of Niebuhr's philosophy, clearly testifying to the 'negative' conception of order to which he subscribed, 'in the field of collective behaviour the force of egoistic passion is so strong that the only harmonies possible are those which manage to neutralise a rival force through balances of power, through mutual defences against its inordinate expression'.[40]

It was precisely the fear that, in a nuclear context, force could no longer be used to neutralise force that led to anxiety that international order would thereby be undermined. Accordingly, it is not at all surprising that one of the major tasks of post-1945 realism has been the elaboration of strategic doctrines appropriate to the nuclear age in which the 'utility' of military power would be preserved even if its 'usability' had been called into question. In other words, for the sake of international order, the Clausewitzian war system had to be maintained even if technological conditions had changed: the injunction *para bellum* must still have meaning because without it, how can a 'neutralised' order be sustained? Thus Kissinger, in writing his major contribution on the impact of nuclear weaponry, saw the purpose of strategic studies in the following terms: 'In seeking to avoid the horrors of all-out war by outlining an alternative, in developing a concept of limitation that combines firmness with moderation, diplomacy can once more establish a relationship with force even in the nuclear age.'[41] If the prop of order is to be threatened violence, then it follows that the task of the logician of strategy, confronted with nuclear weaponry, is to restore credibility to such threats.

The third dimension of twentieth-century realist thought is a culmination of, and a combination of, the other two. It is also the aspect of recent realist thought that has been most frequently misunderstood. It has often been suggested that attempts to integrate 'power' with 'morality' in international politics represent a departure from the pure realist tradition. In one sense, this is true but only if we consider the entire realist tradition to derive from Machiavelli or Hobbes. If, instead, we take Rousseau to be representative of an alternative realist tradition, then the effort to define the place of morality within the realm of international politics, and the resultant despair at the inability to integrate the two adequately, is the twentieth-century realist tradition *par excellence* and not a deviation from it. It is in this specific sense that Rousseau's relevance to the present century is to be appreciated.

There are various ways of making this point. At one level, it has been argued by some that there is a school of realist thought that, while accepting power as a means, rejects it as an ultimate end. Rousseau himself would obviously be encompassed within

this approach. Another way of saying this might be that the hypnotic realist chant that 'all politics is power politics' should be heard as a cry of moral anguish and not as a public celebration of the amoralities of *Realpolitik*. No one has provided a more incisive account of the 'realities' of international politics than did Rousseau himself; this did not, however, prevent him from deploring what he saw.

It is this despair, that there is a moral realm as well as one of power but an inability to reconcile the two, that is the most characteristic trait of twentieth-century realism. It is manifest in almost every realist analyst of international politics who has made a contribution to the discipline in the last few decades.

Nowhere is this better illustrated than in the writings of Reinhold Niebuhr. He was preoccupied by the dualism of human nature and the corresponding potentialities for good and evil displayed within the political universe – with the interplay between the 'light' and the 'dark'. As Thompson has observed 'the heart of Niebuhr's criticism is that modern views of man which stress exclusively either his dignity or his misery are fatuous and irrelevant as they fail to consider the good and evil, the dualism in man's nature'.[42] This duality in man, and the ambivalence of his political enterprises, becomes starker, and its potential consequences more dangerous, with increases in man's power: 'it should have been obvious long before the nuclear age that the mastery over natural forces increased man's power; and that this greater power could be used – and in a sense was bound to be used – destructively as well as creatively'.[43]

Likewise, E. H. Carr, who berated the post-1918 generation of utopians for neglecting the fact of power in international relations, ended up in a moral *impasse* no less agonising than that experienced by Rousseau. Having demolished the utopian edifice, Carr also draws attention to the limitations of realism and urges upon us the classical *via media*, a projected synthesis of the two. Likewise, while he has denied that universal moral principles can be applied to international politics, he nonetheless attempts in *The Twenty Years' Crisis* to find a place for morality as well as for power. He does not succeed and he, no less than his readers, must have been dissatisfied with the compromise at which he arrives. Underneath Carr's proferred solution, one

cannot avoid detecting the same despair that strikes one in the pages of Rousseau. Nowhere is Carr's agony better conveyed than in the following passage:

Having demolished the current utopia with the weapons of realism we still need to build a new utopia of our own, which will one day fall to the same weapons. The human will, will continue to seek an escape from the logical consequences of realism in the vision of an international order which, as soon as it crystallises itself into concrete political form, becomes tainted with self-interest and hypocrisy, and must once more be attacked with the instruments of realism.[44]

One commentator upon Carr, on the basis of such passages, goes on to argue that 'it is this "vision of an international order", this search for principles, which can give moral meaning and set normative limits to the struggle for power on the international scene, that sets Carr apart from the realist school of thought ... in its pure form'.[45] The argument depends upon how we define the 'pure form' of realism but, as mentioned above, if we accept Rousseau as a precursor of an equally important tradition of realism, Carr is within its mainstream and need not be 'set apart'.

With Morgenthau, it seems at first that we are back to 'pure' realism. And yet, even in this case, it can be seen that Morgenthau is concerned with the tragedy of international politics and not simply with revelling in *Realpolitik* for its own sake. Walter Lippmann has been quoted as describing Morgenthau as 'the most moral man I know',[16] and Thompson himself refers to 'Morgenthau's essentially tragic view of the course of action open to statesmen'.[47]

Morgenthau perceives the same dilemma that had beset Rousseau, namely that there are certain moral goals to which mankind should aspire but that there are exigencies of international politics in a world of 'crazy' men that render it difficult, if not futile, to try to realise them. Morgenthau himself gave expression to this tension:

Political realism is aware of the moral significance of political action. It is also aware of the ineluctable tension between the moral command and the requirements of successful political action. And it is unwilling to gloss over and obliterate that tension and thus to obfuscate both the moral and the political issue by making it appear as though the stark facts of politics were morally more satisfying than they actually are, and the moral law less exacting than it actually is.[48]

Finally, in this rapid survey of twentieth-century realism, we can again re-emphasise that its most distinctive refrain has been that of reconciliation between opposites, between power and morality, and a subsequent anguish at its incapacity to perform this task satisfactorily. Most recently, for instance, the attempt to achieve a synthesis, or at least an appeal that such a synthesis is necessary, has been made by K. Thompson.[49] In this sense, Rousseau's dilemma, that there should be a solution to the problem of international order but that none is available, still haunts the twentieth-century mind.

REALISM AND 'NECESSITY'

Realism, like utopianism, makes appeal to necessity. And yet, as in the previous chapter, we are forced to consider whether the necessity resides 'in the events' themselves or whether it merely denotes a 'degree of belief'. Again, as with the utopians, there must be a strong suspicion that the necessity that is invoked to bolster the realist case is of the latter kind.

The necessity that figures in the realist account is the demands upon the statesman operating within a world of unchanging power politics. As such, necessity is for the realist a conservative force rather than the revolutionary agent that it has been considered to be by utopians. The necessity that transfuses the realist world is one that binds the statesman to the existing international order because of the dangers of the unknown.

'Necessity' as the conserver of the power-political mode of operating the international system has been a permanent feature of realist thought, most obviously expressed in its Machiavellian variant. It can perhaps be best demonstrated in terms of the political necessity under which the statesman must function:

Thus what makes any reform apparently impossible is the profound and pessimistic conviction (rooted in the instincts, and borne out by histori- cal experience) to the effect that it is not possible to improve the character of state activity. The Idealist will always be repeating his demand for such a reform and will always be declaring it to be possible. The responsible and executive statesman ... will always find himself constrained by the pressure of the responsibility he bears for the whole to doubt the possibility of it, and to take up a line of conduct that is in accordance with this doubt.[50]

The statesman, if he wishes to be successful, is compelled to take notice of the laws of power politics and not to stray from them. Thus Kissinger reflects the conservatism of realist necessity when he provides his admonition against attempts at utopia-building: 'The statesman must remain forever suspicious of these efforts, not because he enjoys the pettiness of manipulation, but because he must be prepared for the worst contingency.'[51] He was subsequently to write of the role of the statesman in the same conservative vein:

his first goal is survival; he feels responsible not only for the best but also for the worst conceivable outcome. His view of human nature is wary; he is conscious of many great hopes which have failed, of many good intentions that could not be realised, of selfishness and ambition and violence. He is, therefore, inclined to erect hedges against the possibility that even the most brilliant idea might prove abortive.[52]

We have here a necessity that is quite different from that which functions as the engine of transformation in the utopian dialectic. The realist necessity is one that ensures that statesmen will always play according to the perennial rules of the game. Thus a chapter of one realist tract is entitled significantly 'The Limits of Principle in International Politics: Necessity and the New Balance of Power'.[53]

Some caution is required, however, in our understanding of the sense in which realist necessity acts as a 'conservative' force. This does not mean that realist policies are set implacably against any form of innovation. Indeed, necessity may itself, in the name of realism, require the adoption of 'revolutionary' techniques. This is amply revealed in a telling quotation from Niebuhr about the early development of nuclear weapons: 'No nation will fail to take even the most hazardous adventure into the future, if the alternative of not taking the step means the risk of being subjugated.'[54] The point to be emphasised is that realism is conservative of the general order that prevails in international life, not about the specific modalities by means of which that order is sustained. Thus nuclear weapons, although in technological terms they may be considered revolutionary, are to be used to conserve an order based upon the counterbalancing of force against force.

The argument that realist 'necessity', no less than the utopian, represents a 'degree of belief' is reinforced when we highlight a

central paradox or inconsistency within the heart of realism itself. The paradox is this. On the one hand, realist doctrine asserts a claim to objective understanding of the processes of international politics: it is only in terms of such an understanding that the realist can perceive a necessity to which the statesman is bound. Realists, therefore, much more than utopians speak with an air of certitude about politics, because they believe it to be governed by immutable laws, deriving either from human nature itself or from the dynamics of inter-state competition. It is, after all, Morgenthau's proud claim that 'the concept of interest defined as power imposes intellectual discipline upon the observer, infuses rational order into the subject matter of politics, and thus makes the theoretical understanding of politics possible'.[55] Realism is, therefore, closely identified with unshakeable knowledge about how states have behaved and will continue to behave.

On the other hand, it is impossible not to detect in much realist writing, a radical uncertainty that is itself offered as the justification for cautious and conservative practices in international affairs. It is precisely because he is uncertain as to how other states are going to behave that the statesman must be on his guard and, in Kissinger's terminology, 'prepared for the worst contingency'. Not for nothing is a realist approach to national security affairs associated with 'worst-case' planning – with the idea that national strategy should be predicated upon an assumption that the worst may happen and that states should be prepared for it – and this mentality clearly derives, not from the certitudes of international politics but precisely from its uncertainties. Accordingly, it comes as no surprise to see realists arguing that 'foreign policy is at least three-fourths guesswork'[56] and that 'world politics is an incalculable process'.[57] In the light of this radical uncertainty, the necessity to which realists make appeal becomes increasingly difficult to discover.

Finally, that realism, no less than utopianism, reflects a 'degree of belief' is suggested by the following considerations. The fundamental assumption of realism, the one from which its very name derives, is that there is such a thing as an objectively real world of international politics and that its characteristics are given and knowable. But how can we know what that reality is? How can we be sure that the realists, because of their image of

the world, are not the prisoners of their own artificial reality, which they have themselves created? As one writer has expressed it:

There developed after the Second World War a school of 'political realists' who argued that the facts of aggressiveness and power should be recognised, and that 'idealism' in the form of functional co-operation was misplaced. The 'proof' was war. What the 'political realists' failed to appreciate was that an assumption of aggressiveness, and the organisation of world society into power blocs, would inevitably lead to defensive and aggressive responses that would lead to war. Nothing was 'proved' except that certain policies invoke certain responses. If the intentions of governments were security and peace, then their strategic policies were self-defeating – they brought about just those conditions they were intended to prevent.[58]

The full significance of this suggestion deserves to be pondered. If we push such reasoning to its ultimate conclusion then it leads to no less than the total obliteration of the distinction between realism and utopianism. It becomes uncertain who are the 'realists' and who are the 'utopians' because they are both the creators of an international order based upon an idea of what that order is and what it might be. Indeed, in a sense, it could be argued that it is the realists who are the truly successful utopians because they have created a world after their own image. Could there be any more wonderful tribute to the potency of ideas in human affairs? Lewis Mumford has seized upon this reversion of roles, that it is the realists who are the genuine utopians, and developed the theme in a powerful passage. He deserves to have the last word:

Utopian idealists who have overestimated the power of the ideal are plainly much more fully in possession of their senses and more closely linked to human realities than the scientific and military 'realists' who have turned the use of absolute weapons into a compulsive ideal . . . The leaders of science, technology, and military affairs who have most despised the function of ideals have actually turned the expansion of their equipment for destruction and extermination into an ultimate ideal. This is utopianism with a vengeance: the nihilistic perfection of nothingness.[59]

Part II

The practice of international order

4 *From balance to Concert: 1815–1854*

As students of international politics, our interest in the congress system and in the Concert of Europe hinges on an attempt to see these diplomatic techniques in the broad perspective of their contribution to the theory and practice of international relations. That is to say that the questions that mainly concern us are the following: Was there such a thing as the Concert of Europe? Did it survive beyond the period of congress diplomacy in the few years after the 1815 settlement? Upon what principles if any was the Concert based? To what extent was the Concert a novel element in the history of international relations? These are the kinds of question that will be discussed in the course of this chapter.

There are two main themes in modern international history – themes that are frequently confused but ought to be kept apart. The one is the development of international organisation, the construction of an institutional framework within which independent sovereign states might interact: its focus is upon diplomatic machinery. The other is the assertion of a special managerial role for the Great Powers in the shaping of international order: its focus is upon diplomatic norms. Moreover, it is one of the principal deficiencies of the 'whig' interpretation of international history that it has mistaken the latter process for evidence of the vitality of the former. But not only are the two processes distinct: they are, indeed, in some fundamental sense antagonistic and, far from suggesting a unilinear concept of progress in state behaviour, they may be interpreted – normatively – as symptoms of a duality in historical development in which 'progressive' elements are counterbalanced by 'regressive' ones. If the former process is regarded as an expression of the

utopian impulse in international affairs, then the latter is surely the consummation of realist demands.

Nowhere is this deep-seated confusion more apparent than in scholarly discussion of the Concert of Europe. It is evident in the historical parallels in terms of which commentators explain the Concert, it being depicted as the historical precursor of the League of Nations and of the United Nations. Unfortunately, to describe the European Concert in such a manner is to miss the major significance of the first half of the nineteenth century as a phase in the development of international politics. Rather than see the United Nations as the heritage of Concert experience, we should more minimally see the structure of the Security Council in that role, or, perhaps even more appropriately, the 'conventions of crisis' that some analysts discern in the recent behaviour of the Super-Powers.[1] This is to say that the significance of the Concert lies in its elaboration of rules of diplomatic conduct for the Great Powers and only tangentially in its contribution to the theory of international organisation. The historian who sees the incipient phase of the Concert, in the shape of the Congress system, as occupying 'in man's quest for peace through international conferences and organizations a position which is almost midway between Emeric Cruce's *Nouveau Cynée* (1623) and the United Nations of contemporary fame'[2] is, therefore, well wide of the mark.

The confusion is neatly captured in yet another commentary. The authors of this work argue at one point that 'the Munich Conference of September 1938 can be described as the last great meeting of the old Concert of Europe'.[3] Whatever the historical accuracy of extending the life of the Concert into the twentieth century, the authors are surely correct in perceiving the essence of the Concert to lie in the mode of Great-Power management of the international system. Subsequently, however, the same authors obscure the issue by presenting the following summary: 'Taking nineteenth- and twentieth-century international relations as a whole it is evident that the traditions of conference or parliamentary diplomacy is a growing one. The informal Concert of Europe gave way to the League of Nations and that in its turn gave place to the much stronger UN.'[4] Here, once again, the focus has shifted back from norms to machinery.

In essence, the significance of the Concert derives from two inter-related ideas. The first of these was the formal assertion of the unique privileges and responsibilities of the Great Powers in the maintenance of international order. The second, made necessary by the first, was that if the special managerial role of the Great Powers was to be recognised, it would be necessary to 'order' more formally the relationships between the powers themselves. It is from this dual perspective, as both asserting a special role for the Great Powers and then attempting to mitigate some of the consequences of this, that the unique contribution of the Concert is to be appreciated and its supercession of a crude balance-of-power system to be understood.

These two facets of the Concert system have, indeed, been highlighted by historians of the period. Of the former, Elrod has observed that 'concert diplomacy actively cultivated the conception of the great powers as a unique and special peer group',[5] echoing Albrecht-Carrié's assessment of the rationale of the Concert that 'order could best be maintained by the clear assertion of the right and responsibility of those possessed of power, the Great Powers'.[6] Of the latter, Elrod has likewise drawn attention to the Concert as 'a conceptual norm among the great powers of the proper and permissible aims and methods of international politics',[7] or more simply put, the Concert was a 'group norm'.[8]

Although speaking of a different period, Medlicott is intuitively aware of these two dimensions of the Concert idea. In a comment upon Gladstone's attempted revival of Concert diplomacy later in the century, Medlicott comments that Gladstone did not seem to distinguish between 'the Concert as a tutelage of the great powers over the smaller, and the Concert as a means of preserving the peace of Europe by preventing war between the great powers themselves'.[9] The Concert, therefore, was *of* the powers and *between* the powers.

Reverting to the above distinction between the Concert as a contribution to the norms of Great-Power behaviour and the Concert as a forerunner of international organisations of this century, we discover that such a distinction helps to make sense of the apparently inconsistent judgements of historians upon the Concert in another respect. For some, as will be discussed shortly,

the keynote of the Concert was its attempt to formalise inter-national politics, to systematise a spontaneous balance-of-power situation: for others, by contrast, the keynote of the Concert is its informal nature, to the point where its very existence has been called into question. As Holbraad was to put it 'at its best, it might be described as an informal institution; at its worst, as non-existent'.[10]

Some of the resultant confusion is dissipated if we recollect the terms in which the formality or the informality of the Concert is being judged. To those who look to the Concert in terms of a lineage of organisational development – as diplomatic machinery – the Concert is, to be sure, informal, as there was no regularity of meeting and no permanent apparatus. In a more important sense, however, the Concert did formalise rules of Great-Power behaviour and if we look to the Concert for diplomatic norms, rather than diplomatic machinery, the rewards are more ob-viously tangible. In other words, to characterise, and implicitly to criticise, the Concert as an informal organisation is as true as it is irrelevant because the Concert never aspired to organisational status in our understanding of that word.

Inis Claude is aware of this distinction but, perhaps surpris-ingly in a book on the development of international organi-sations,[11] his references to it are implicit rather than explicit. In discussing the Concert, Claude comments that 'the political conference system . . . produced the prototype of a major organ of modern international organisation – the executive council of the great powers'.[12] What he fails to stress is that although the development of modern international organisations has coincided with the notion of Great-Power tutelage, there was no necessary nexus between them (even if there were strong 'realistic' reasons for the coincidence) and the history of the former should not be equated with the history of the latter. The evolution of Great-Power norms of behaviour has, in other words, been a discrete development, and even if modern international organisations have chosen to incorporate these norms into a 'major organ', we can nonetheless imagine Great-Power adherence to these norms outside an organisational setting[13] just as we can imagine inter-national organisations that would not embody these norms.

In attempting to assess the nature and the novelty of the

Concert of Europe, the first question to be answered is whether or not the diplomatic code established in 1815 was significantly different from that which had existed prior to 1789. In other words, is it possible to view the structure of post-1815 international politics as no more than a return to the principles which had guided European diplomats in the years before the French Revolution, principles that had been violated by the Napoleonic wars? This question may be tackled by trying to introduce a further distinction, that between the Concert of Europe as a diplomatic mechanism and the balance of power as it had operated in eighteenth-century international relations.

That the Concert was based upon a stable balance of power there can be little dispute: that it went beyond the practices of the balance is not universally agreed. Nonetheless, there are reasons for believing that a valid distinction can be made between the two. Schroeder, certainly, is of the opinion that 'what accounted for European peace after 1815 was rather a system of international order established upon a balance of power, *but going well beyond it*'.[14] Likewise, Elrod is convinced, and I think correctly so, that 'the Concert derived from the common realization of European statesmen of the Napoleonic era that something new and different must be devised to mitigate the increasingly chaotic and warlike balance-of-power system of the previous century'.[15]

At first sight, this is a view that may not commend itself. Most commentators would agree that the Concert of Europe was in some important sense linked with the post-war congress system and similarly most historians would be forced to concede that the congress system of diplomacy had its origins in the wartime coalitions brought together to oppose Napoleon. In other words, at first sight, the Concert of Europe seems to derive its historical lineage directly from what was one of the most salient examples of the balance-of-power doctrine in practice. The wars had seen a succession of alliances and coalitions in which the European powers combined to thwart the pretensions of revolutionary and Napoleonic France.

Moreover, the principle of balance that had guided the European powers in their efforts to check French preponderance was visibly carried into the territorial settlement itself. This can be seen in several aspects of the settlement. Most notably it can

be seen to apply to the provisions that concerned France. Many analysts have drawn attention to the principle, hallowed in balance-of-power doctrine, that deviant states should be restored to their former standing in international society. This principle was certainly observed in relation to France. France was largely restored to her pre-revolutionary boundaries and, although she had to submit to an indemnity and to an occupation army for a short period, she was otherwise readmitted as the traditional French actor on the international stage. To have done otherwise would have placed an artificial constraint on the workings of the balance-of-power mechanism.

The territorial provisions of the Vienna settlement, as they related to France, displayed adherence to the balance principle in another sense. Since France had challenged Europe and attempted to establish predominance, measures were taken to prevent a recurrence of this development. This is clearly illustrated in the alterations to the map of Europe along France's eastern border. In the north, Belgium and Holland were united to pose a more powerful buffer state against possible future French expansion. Further south, Prussia's position on the Rhineland was strengthened, again as a check to France. Further south again, the permanent neutralisation of Switzerland was guaranteed by the signatories to the settlement. And in the extreme south, Austria's position in Italy was enhanced by the acquisition of Venice.

Traditional balance-of-power manouevres were characteristic of the Vienna Congress in yet another sense. The most contentious issue to be settled at the Congress was the Polish question. This problem soon produced a clear alignment between the powers. Russia sought to swallow up most of Poland and Prussia was prepared to agree to this provided that she was similarly allowed to swallow up the whole of Saxony. This neither Britain nor Austria could permit. Consequently, France, supposed to be the defeated party and not a framer of the settlement, was called into the balance mechanism and, choosing to support Britain and Austria, was instrumental in forcing both Russia and Prussia to limit their aims.

Was the Concert of Europe no more, then, than the re-establishment of the traditional balance-of-power system? There seems to be some ground for saying so. We have just seen how the

balance principle underlay the anti-Napoleonic coalitions and in fact permeated the entire Vienna settlement. And it is equally clear that if the Concert of Europe was anything at all it was the offspring of the very coalition that had produced the Vienna settlement. More specifically, if the Concert of Europe referred to any concrete diplomatic method, it was the one that had its origins in the provisions of the Quadruple Alliance of 1814, reaffirmed in November 1815. As a product of their wartime experience, which (the allies argued) had been successful in managing the war, the European powers agreed in this document to attempt to manage the peace in the post-1815 period. As the sixth article of the Quadruple Alliance stated:

> To facilitate and to secure the execution of the present treaty and to consolidate the connections which at the present moment so closely unite the Four Sovereigns for the happiness of the World, the High Contracting Parties have agreed to renew their meetings at fixed periods ... for the purpose of consulting upon their common interests and for the consideration of the measures which at each of these periods shall be considered the most salutary for the repose and prosperity of Nations and for the maintenance of the Peace of Europe.

It was this statement of intent that gave birth to the series of periodic congresses that characterised European diplomatic history for the next few years and, intermittently, throughout most of the century.

While we have shown that the treaty and the Congress that established the practice of congress diplomacy were themselves to a large extent products of balance-of-power philosophy, it can be argued that if the Concert of Europe was anything at all, it was something more than the traditional balance-of-power system.

This is not a view that would be shared by everyone. Indeed there are strong historical arguments against it. Carsten Holbraad in his excellent study of British and German ideas on the Concert of Europe has identified a school of thought that he has labelled 'the balance of power' for the simple reason that this school thought of the Concert of Europe solely as an instrument of balance-of-power diplomacy. Nevertheless it can be argued that the main contribution of the Concert of Europe to diplomatic theory and practice was precisely its modifications of the balance of power. This is the very essence of the idea of the Concert of Europe.

The emergence of the European Concert is closely related to, but not identical with, two developments within balance-of-power theory itself. The first of these relates to the process by means of which balance is achieved; the second pertains to the type of equilibrium that is sought.

As regards the first of these developments, balance-of-power theory was already undergoing, late in the eighteenth century, a transformation that would remove from it many of its naturalistic assumptions. The point has been well made by M. Wright:

The pervasiveness of natural analogues was derived from a tradition of thought which assumed the universality of the Laws of Nature. Human affairs were part of nature and subject to its laws ... the transition from a naturalistic to an artificial conception of the balance of power is a gradual one and to some extent parallels the transition from natural to positive theories of international law.[16]

The balance of power was, in other words, becoming increasingly recognised as a product of human contrivance rather than as a gift of nature and the Concert reflected this development. Wright himself makes this point:

Although the solidarity and cooperation of the Concert of Europe have often been exaggerated, it recognised, at least in theory, that the balance of power required a more conscious, rational management.[17]

The nature of the equilibrium upon which the Concert was to rest was also different from that which had characterised the eighteenth century: its fundamental concept was, according to Gulick,[18] the coalition rather than the alliance. As Gulick has expressed it, 'this coalition equilibrium, or Concert, became the institutional adjustment of the European state system to the new multiple balance and the inadequacy of the older system of alliance balance'.[19] He elaborates:

The years 1812–15 are especially meaningful to the student of the balance of power for the further reason that they witnessed the temporary evolution of a coalition equilibrium from the antecedent, eigth-teenth century system of alliance balance. The wars of the French Revolution and Napoleonic dominion had provided the terrible anvil upon which coalitions were forged; and the statesmen of the great powers attempted to consummate their experience of wartime coalitions by the creation of an automatic coalition which would solve the problem of enforcement for the state system in the postwar period.[20]

But the Concert was to be more than a simple revision of balance doctrine. First, we can agree with the view of Hinsley in his study *Power and the Pursuit of Peace* that the post-Vienna period of international politics was characterised as much by a reaction against traditional balance-of-power politics as by attempts to adhere to the principles of the balance doctrine. If the powers of Europe felt that the balance mechanism was still a necessary element in the proper functioning of the European state system, they no longer seemed so convinced that it was a sufficient principle upon which to order their relations with each other. This should not be overstated. There was not the same moral reaction against power politics in 1815 as was to be demonstrated in 1918. Nonetheless, although the degree was different, the same sentiment was there in embryo. Although the balance of power might preserve the state system, there emerged the beginnings of the feeling that it was not the most efficient way of achieving this end and that perhaps some other mechanism should be relied upon to provide the order thought desirable in the conduct of inter-state relations.

In consequence the essence of the Concert of Europe was to add an extra embellishment onto the operation of the balance system. Not only should the mechanism operate, but its operations should be sanctioned and legitimised by the European Concert of Great Powers.

How did this work in practice? For the few years subsequent upon the Vienna settlement, and on the precedent established by Vienna itself, the characteristic mode of operation of the European Concert was the Congress. At Vienna, not only was the European balance of power restored but the distribution of power that emerged from the territorial settlement was legitimised by agreement of the powers. Similarly, when in 1818 the allies decided that the occupation army could be withdrawn from France and France fully readmitted to her previous international status by being allowed to join the Quadruple Alliance, these deeds were legitimised by a congress at Aix-la-Chapelle. The rationale behind the powers' decision to readmit France to full membership of the system was based on traditional European doctrine. As the 1818 protocol itself was to state, 'assuring to France the place that belongs to her in the European system, will

bind her more closely to the pacific and benevolent views in which all the sovereigns participate and will thus consolidate the general tranquillity'. But although the reasoning was traditional, the method employed to achieve this end was novel. France did not just resume her place in Europe as an inevitable fact of nature. Rather she was admitted by a formal document – the product of a general meeting of the Great Powers.

We can, then, concur with Hinsley in what he considers to be the two main principles of the Concert of Europe – the two principles that give substance to the idea of the Concert of Europe and distinguish it from the diplomatic procedures of other periods of international history. These were:

(1) that the Great Powers had a common responsibility for maintaining the territorial *status quo* of the treaties of 1815 and for solving the international problems that arose in Europe; and

(2) that when the *status quo* had to be modified or a problem had to be settled, changes should not be made unilaterally and gains should not be made without their formal and common consent.[21]

It was this requirement of 'formal and common consent' that most clearly distinguishes the Concert of Europe from the simple workings of the balance of power. As has been said, in the immediate post-1815 period, the diplomatic instrument by means of which this formal and common consent was sought was the Congress of the powers.

Of course, there was no unanimity between the powers as to the purpose to which these congresses should be put and clear divisions soon appeared that indicated the internal strains of the system. Moreover, in order to understand these strains, it is first necessary to look at the common interests upon which the powers thought that the Concert of Europe was based.

Here there were divisions from the very beginning, divisions that were to become increasingly conspicuous the more the powers tried to use the congress mechanism in practice. All the powers shared a feeling that it was the duty of the major states of Europe to ensure that international order prevailed on the continent. Unfortunately, they did not share a common conception of what constituted international order.

For Britain, separated by water from continental Europe and with major interests lying outside Europe itself, the main pre-occupation in the post-war years was in preserving the territorial settlement of 1815 and the territorial balance of power that this settlement had set out to achieve. In other words, as far as Castlereagh was concerned, international order was precisely that – a problem that began and ended at state frontiers.

Not so for Metternich, the Austrian Chancellor. In common with many leading conservative statesmen of the time, Metternich came increasingly to define international order in terms of internal domestic conditions. Had not the international upheaval of the 1793–1815 period sprung from the internal events in France? In other words, as far as Metternich was concerned, there was no point in preserving simply the structure of the 1815 state system if this structure could in turn be overthrown by domestic upheavals. The powers must concern themselves as much with internal developments within states as with external frontiers.

Metternich's concern did not lie with the state system alone. He was also, as the Austrian Chancellor, concerned with dynastic rights. Consequently he was opposed to revolutions, to con-stitutionalism, to nationalism, on two main grounds: first, be-cause they represented a threat to international order; and secondly, but perhaps more importantly, because they repre-sented an immediate threat to the Habsburg Empire itself. If any state had reason to fear the principles of the revolution and the emerging principles of nationalism it was the Habsburg Empire, which was vulnerable on every count.

Flowing from these two perceptions of respective national interests, the British and the Austrian, there emerged two views on the functions of international congresses. For Metternich, the states of Europe must act conjointly to stamp out the internal threats to international security. The image that he appealed to was that of a universal conspiracy. Europe should view itself not as divided vertically into states but as divided horizontally into rulers, on the one hand, and revolutionaries on the other. It was the collective duty of all the states to stamp out this revolutionary contagion before it could spread and before it could present another challenge to Europe's international arrangements. In the

words of one historian, the monarchs of Europe must hang together if they were not to hang separately. This was the justification for international intervention in internal affairs – precisely the reasoning that was to underlie the interventions in the Russian civil war, following upon 1917.

Again, Europe should not be regarded as having been divided into two rigid camps over this issue. Broadly speaking there was an alignment of the autocratic powers of the east, Russia, Prussia and Austria on the one hand, and the constitutional powers of the west, Britain and France on the other. However, these were in no sense solid alliances. Despite the Holy Alliance that, ostensibly at least, bound the eastern powers, Austria and Prussia had a serious conflict of interest over which state should have preponderance in Germany, and Austria and Russia had a serious conflict of interest in the Balkans. Similarly, Britain and France were, throughout the nineteenth century, to find themselves at cross-purposes over Egypt. The continent was not therefore split into two hard-and-fast ideological camps. Nor were Castlereagh's views basically more liberal than those of Metternich. They were just as conservative, although about slightly different things. This is a point which Carsten Holbraad has made well in his book on *The Concert of Europe:*

The British conservative idea was about an alliance of great powers established by treaties and formal declarations not a union of sovereigns founded in common sentiments and interests; about the external freedom of the members of the states system, not the internal condition of the parts of the society of Europe; about the threat of aggression not the danger of revolution. But the essence of the idea was conservative: preservation of the boundaries that the statesmen of 1815 had drawn in an attempt to balance the powers of Europe.

These divisions emerged more starkly in the remaining congresses of the period – those at Troppau, Laibach and Verona, convened to discuss the revolutions in Naples, Sicily and Spain. Although the powers could not at these meetings come to an agreement on joint action to suppress these revolutions, that is probably of more interest to the historian. The point of major interest is that the powers felt it necessary to summon congresses – and, let it be remembered, actually succeeded in convening these congresses – in order to deal with problems that were

thought to be important for the peace of Europe. It is this idea, that the individual powers should not take unilateral action on questions important to the whole of the continent, that was the underlying reality of the Concert of Europe and its most distinctive contribution to the functioning of international politics in the nineteenth century.

Perhaps one more point should be made at this juncture. There were two broad reasons why diplomacy by congress or by conference achieved the success that it did at this period. One was undoubtedly that there was no major and urgent issue to be resolved between any two of the major powers. The Great Powers find it easiest to co-operate when they are jointly imposing a settlement on some third party, preferably a smaller state. This is a characteristic of Great-Power behaviour as conspicuous in the present day as in the nineteenth century. However, when it comes to a direct conflict between two major powers, co-operation is not so easily achieved. So, in a sense, the Concert of Europe was, perhaps, not much more than the negative expression of the fact that for the time being the Great Powers of Europe could live with the differences between them. There was no burning issue that cried out for an immediate settlement.

There is another reason, one that has already been referred to. That the Great Powers were cautious in the post-1815 period, and refrained from pressing their mutual differences to the point of conflict, can be partially explained by the internal condition of the major powers and especially of Austria. The French Revolution had taught a lesson that was to be repeated in 1830 and again in 1848, that the social order of Europe was fragile and it would not require much of a push to knock it down. For countries with one eye on the internal situation, this was no time for international adventures.

It is this 'negative' view of the Concert that Medlicott has encapsulated in his dictum that 'it was peace that maintained the Concert, and not the Concert that maintained peace'.[22] In consequence, it was the forces operating for peace that created the illusion of a successful Concert and not the Concert that produced stability, a view echoed in Northedge's dismissal of the peace-keeping role of the Concert as working 'quite simply, because the international system as a whole was oriented towards

the maintenance of peace at the core'.[23] Elrod is one of the few who regard the Concert in 'positive' terms as an 'essential ingredient of European peace and stability between the Congress of Vienna and the Crimean War'.[24]

What are we to make of these rival interpretations? In a sense, the argument is a chicken-and-egg one and, as such, resistant to a satisfactory conclusion: even if the underlying conditions favoured Concert diplomacy, the functioning of the Concert might nonetheless have reinforced the inherent tendencies towards international stability. In any case, there is one important respect in which the answer to that question is immaterial. Even if we accept that the contribution of the Concert to peace-maintenance was minimal, this need not imply that no Concert was in existence nor that our interest in the Concert is thereby diminished: to do so is to assume that the Concert's principal *raison d'être* was peace-maintenance and that our only interest in studying norms of international political behaviour is to determine how they enhance the prospects for peace. But peace and war are more often the byproducts of international activities rather than their proximate goals. To put it in its starkest form: the Concert is of interest primarily as a set of norms associated with the process of Great-Power decision-making at the international level; whether that process was a peaceful one is of enormous human import but comes second in the order of study. We must carefully delineate the essential features of the process before (optionally) moving on to consider its operational consequences.

Another way of making the same point might be to reintroduce the distinction, referred to earlier, between international order as process and international order as substance. The Concert of Europe was a conscious process of regulating Great-Power behaviour by requiring that it should be conducted within the terms of the 'formal and common consent' formula. It was, in that sense, a contribution to order, if not to peace.

The main question that remains to be answered is, how long the Concert continued to function as a significant feature of international politics?

As we have so far identified the Concert of Europe closely with the congress system, there is the possibility that the Concert of Europe disappeared with the eclipse of the congress system. Most

historians are agreed that the year 1822, in which the Congress of Verona was held, was the last episode in the history of the congress system, as there was no other congress held until 1856 and only one more after that in 1878. So does that mean that the Concert of Europe died a premature death in 1822? This would be a misreading of the situation because although the Congress as an international diplomatic instrument disappeared from the scene for over thirty years, the powers did not abandon the practice of legitimising changes to the international order through the mechanism of international procedures, usually taking the form of international conferences.

These conferences bear witness to the continuing concern of the powers to modify the workings of the pure balance-of-power system by making it a cardinal principle that changes in the balance of power, or territorial adjustments likely to have consequences for the balance of power, must receive the formal sanction of the powers and must not occur as unilateral actions.

This clearly happened in the instances of Belgian and Greek independence. The separation of Belgium from Holland was the first major revision of the 1815 settlement and it was achieved by the common consent of the Concert meeting in conference and signing a joint document of guarantee. Similarly Greece was recognised as an independent state by a European conference. An agreement on the international legal status of the maritime passage of the Bosphorus was likewise achieved in 1841. Once again, it should be made quite clear that there was no great unanimity of the powers on all these questions. Agreements, or compromises, were arrived at only after protracted negotiation. It would be quite wrong to conclude that during this period the European powers provided an outstanding example of harmony and good will. Nothing could be further from the truth. At the same time, they did see fit to adopt a procedure of international legitimisation of change and to moderate their rivalries in order to accommodate such a procedure. And it is important that this fact too should not be ignored.

If the Concert survived beyond 1822, what then is its date of termination? This is, of course, of more than historical interest. Clearly, one's conception of the essential nature of the Concert must change depending on whether the terminal date is said to

be 1822, 1848, 1856, 1878 or 1914. Hinsley is of the opinion that the Concert functioned until 1914 and was then destroyed. Holbraad, too, has traced the evolution of thought on the Concert as far as 1914. There is no reason to doubt that many diplomats and public figures still thought in terms of the Concert of Europe as late as 1914. But, given the principles that we have said lie at the heart of the notion of the Concert of Europe, surely the terminal date must be placed much earlier than this? It will, therefore, be argued that as a diplomatic instrument having a significant effect on European international relations, the Concert of Europe lasted until the mid-1850s.

It has been suggested that the Concert of Europe was a substantial modification of the balance-of-power system in that, while the aims of the powers involved may have been largely unchanged, the diplomatic procedures they employed were novel, the most important of these being the practice of the international legitimisation of change. Viewed in this light, the pivotal episode in the disappearance of the Concert must necessarily be the Crimean War.

This is for the reason that the war was followed by a period, 1859–71, in which the territorial settlement of Vienna was drastically revised. Moreover, this was done unilaterally and by war. The new arrangements were not sanctioned by an international conference or congress. In other words, the map of Europe was redrawn by individual powers without any reference to the 'sense' of a European meeting. If Goodwin is correct in his assessment that 'it was not the Concert that made Europe a reality; rather the Concert was dependent upon it being so',[25] then Europe was no longer a reality after 1856 and the basis of the Concert had been removed.

The territorial readjustments being referred to are, of course, those associated with the unifications of Italy and Germany. The Vienna settlement had gone out of its way to ignore the principle of nationality in its territorial redistribution. The unifications scarcely represented the victory of that principle but rather represented the victory of the tactics of *Realpolitik*. In any case, they entailed a drastic revision of the Vienna arrangements, and by means of war. Further, at the end of each war, settlements were imposed in the traditional manner of European diplomacy.

If in 1866 Bismarck imposed a lenient treaty upon Austria, this was solely out of regard for future Prussian strategy – out of respect for the balance of power, not out of respect for the Concert of Europe.

If we can agree that the Crimean war is the watershed that separates Concert from non-Concert diplomacy, there still remains some historical puzzle over the precise relationship between that war and the operations of the Concert. However, the apparent gulf between some interpretations may not be as wide as a superficial reading suggests or, at least, the theoretical implications of the contrast in interpretations may not be so very important.

Basically, the accounts of the Crimean war (seen in the context of the Concert) fall into two distinct categories, those that see the war as a product of the Concert's performance and those that see it as evidence of the Concert's breakdown. Hinsley subscribes to the former view: 'Far from being able to prevent the Crimean war, the notion of Europe that underlay the Concert was largely responsible for the fact that the war broke out.'[26] Seen in this light, the war was essentially an attempt to make Russia subscribe to Concert rules in the Near East or as Holbraad has put it 'a concert is concerned with maintaining and extending international order rather than with preserving peace'.[27]

Elrod and, to some extent, Schroeder, represent the alternative view. According to Elrod, 'statesmen in key positions failed to exercise self-restraint and refused to honour the rules of the Concert ... The Concert of Europe was the victim. To be sure, remnants of the techniques and assumptions of concert diplomacy endured, but the Concert System itself had been destroyed.'[28] Schroeder's analysis is similar. He contends that 'this destruction of the Concert is the main impact of the Crimean War on the European state system' and makes the further elaboration: 'To say that the war destroyed the Concert is only to say that the Concert failed to prevent the war; its collapse was a consequence of its own failure.'[29]

The arguments are similar to those surrounding the outbreak of the First World War: was the war a product of the balance-of-power system or, alternatively, was the war produced by the failure of the balance mechanism? The problem here seems to be

basically a definitional one in relation to the purposes of a balance system – whether its primary objective is the preservation of peace or whether it is the maintenance of 'equilibrium', or 'stability', or 'order'. If any of the latter, then it may be necessary to resort to war to secure the ends of the system. Accordingly, the 1914–18 war may be viewed as an attempt to preserve the European balance and, as such, as the vindication of the balance system: alternatively, it may be viewed as the failure of the system to prevent war and, as such, as its negation.

The ambivalence of the relationship between the Concert and the Crimean war is similar in kind. It hinges upon our conception of the Concert and whether, as noted above, we are to consider it a peace-preserving or an order-maintaining device. If the former, then the outbreak of the Crimean war may be taken as *prima facie* evidence of the Concert's failure: if the latter, then there is no inconsistency in arguing that the war was a demonstration of an effective Concert.

Whether we pronounce the patient to have died instantaneously in 1854 or to have hung on in a critical condition until the aftermath of the war, there seems no sound basis for doubting that the body of the Concert was truly cold by the late 1850s. Those who have argued that the Concert continued to function throughout the period of Italian and German unifications do so on grounds that are tenuous where they are not confused.

Albrecht-Carrié, for instance, sees the Concert enduring into the immediate pre-1914 period. Unfortunately, the reasons he provides for this assessment are less than convincing. On the 1856–71 period, he has this to say:

The concept of the community of Europe and its orderly functioning through the agency of the Concert was undeniably a reality during the two decades in question. *Nevertheless, the major changes which occurred in this time, the emergence of a united Italy and a similar outcome in Germany, essentially took place without the participation of all Europe* ... The outcome, the appearance of a united Italy, was tacitly accepted by the rest of Europe *without the formality of her collective sanction.*[30]

The problem with such a formulation is that if we take Albrecht-Carrié's qualifications seriously, one wonders what, substantively, remains of the notion of the Concert, because the aspects that he sees as lacking during the 1856–71 period are precisely those

features in terms of which the Concert has been defined. It is tempting, therefore, to point out, as a riposte to Albrecht-Carrié, Medlicott's caustic comment to the effect that 'there was a Concert of Europe when the action of the great powers was concerted, and when it was not there was not'.[31] If less subtle, this nonetheless seems closer to the point.

Albrecht-Carrié's attempts to project the Concert into the post-1870 period are equally strained and depend on an unacceptable degree of equivocation. He insists that the Concert operated after 1870 while conceding that 'the period has a different tone from the preceding part of the century'[32] and later suggests that the alliance system of the pre-1914 era 'while not necessarily a denial of the Concert of Europe, nevertheless has a very different emphasis'.[33] Surely there comes a point where the argument that 'the essence remains even if all visible forms have changed' is detrimental to historical understanding? This is especially true when, as in this case, we are discussing a set of conventions regulating Great-Power behaviour, because such conventions exist only to the extent that they are observed: they cannot be honoured in the breach. Accordingly, it can be argued that rather than pretend that the Concert endures but with a 'different tone' and a 'different emphasis', it is more revealing to speak of the Concert's demise and its replacement by something else.

The Concert of Europe, to the extent that it represented a distinctive contribution to international practice, did so by operating as a modification of the balance-of-power system. It can be contended from this that the Concert of Europe did not function in the latter decades of the nineteenth century for the reason that, far from representing a modification of the balance-of-power system, international politics during the period 1870–1914 reverted to the classic traditions of that system, without embellishment and without refinement. It is to this period that we must now turn.

5 Balance without Concert: 1856–1914

In the previous chapter, the case was presented that in the second half of the nineteenth century, international politics were characterised by a return to pure and simple balance-of-power calculations and this was made the basis of the view that the Concert of Europe ceased to function during this period as, in our definition, the Concert of Europe represented an important departure from balance-of-power policies. In this chapter an attempt will be made to try to demonstrate in what ways the European powers returned to a system of international relations that had more in common, perhaps, with the eighteenth century than with the first half of the nineteenth.

We have to be cautious with our terms. The title of this chapter should not be taken to suggest that there was a balance of power in Europe, in the sense of a distribution of equilibrium, throughout the 1856–1914 period. Manifestly, there were various distributions of power during that period, some more equal than others.[1] For instance, the post-1871 distribution was essentially different from that of 1856–70, if for no other reason than the emergence of a united and powerful Germany at the end of the Franco-Prussian war. Indeed, it is the emergence of Germany that has led historians, like Joll, to refer to a 'new' balance of power after 1870.[2] Likewise, other analysts have perceived a further change in the distribution of power after 1900: for Hinsley, the system lapsed into disequilibrium at the turn of the century.[3]

The statement that international politics between the Crimean and 1914–18 wars were characterised by 'balance' can, therefore, clearly not be interpreted as a claim that there was an unchanging or evenly apportioned distribution of power. The statement relates to something more elementary than this, namely, to the characteristic mode of diplomatic behaviour of the states, and especially of the Great Powers, during this era. Moreover, from this perspective, although Europe experienced substantial war from 1856–71 and then substantial peace from 1871–1914, the

argument of this chapter will be that there was an important continuity in the mode of Great-Power behaviour throughout this entire period, such as to mark the international politics of the post-1856 years off from those of the first half of the nineteenth century. To put it in its most basic form, even if there was no noticeable change in the notions of international order that the states hoped to achieve, there was nonetheless a marked transition in relation to ideas about how that order could best be created or maintained, and that transition may be described as the breakdown of Concert diplomacy and the re-emergence of balance strategies.

Such a contention would by no means receive universal assent. Hinsley's position, for instance, appears at first sight to be diametrically opposed. He says of the post-1870 period:

> It was not solely because of the balance of power, however, that the Powers now reverted to the greater self-restraint of the first half of the nineteenth century. They continued to subscribe to the principles on which a sense of the collectivity of the Powers, of the Concert of Europe, had been based in that earlier period. These principles had survived the recent wars: the continuing tacit acceptance of them was as much the basis of the wide acceptance of the new *status quo* and the common determination to keep the peace after 1871 as was the self-restraint induced by practical considerations arising from the balance of power, though the two factors buttressed each other.[4]

On closer reading, however, it becomes clear that Hinsley's argument for a modified Concert is intended to apply only to the 1870s and, consequently, only for a small portion of our 1856–1914 framework.

The contrary case, and the one which comes closest to the thesis of this chapter, has been cogently expressed by M. S. Anderson:

> This atmosphere of intensified international competition ... meant the end of the concert of Europe as an idea with any effective influence on statesmen. Already weakened by the events of the 1850s and 1860s ... it had by the 1880s become little more than a phantom, a concept to which lip-service might still sometimes be paid but to which no leader of any state any longer owed a serious allegiance ... It was impossible to pretend after 1871 that a France and Germany divided by the unhealed sore of Alsace–Lorraine could ever have, at bottom, common objects, at least in Europe. It was difficult to claim, from the 1880s or 1890s

onwards, that Russia and the Habsburg Empire, increasingly likely to be divided by conflicting ambitions in the Balkans, or Russia and Britain, clearly separated by bitter rivalries in Persia and the Far East, were in a much better position. The dominant characteristic of the diplomacy of the generation which began in the 1870s was the emergence of alliances which divided the major European powers into often competing groups of a closeness and permanence hitherto unknown.[5]

The point then is, in Gulick's terminology, a reversion from the 'coalition equilibrium' of the early part of the century to a system predicated upon a competitive alliance equilibrium. The latter is not a foundation upon which Concert diplomacy can be built.

We have seen that at least as late as the Crimean war of 1854, the major European powers showed an inclination to have revisions of the territorial *status quo* legitimised by some sort of international instrument. However, during the course of the 1850s and 1860s, the map of Europe was radically redrawn without any reference to a European consensus.

From one perspective, it is possible to argue that the fact that this revision was carried out at all was the result of a profound, if temporary, change in the European balance of power. The revolutions of 1848 had undermined any remaining vestiges of the Holy Alliance of the three eastern states, Russia, Prussia and Austria, and of their capacity to act as a conservative check on developments of a revolutionary or nationalistic nature. Metternich had disappeared from the European scene and Austria no longer functioned as the policeman of Europe. The temporary eclipse of the conservative eastern powers from their position as arbiter of the fate of Europe was re-emphasised by the impact of the Crimean war on Russia. That war directed Russia's energies into a period of internal reconstruction and during that time, Russia was less prepared to act as a guardian of the European settlement. The result of all this was that for a short period, Europe was mainly in the hands of Louis Napoleon, the new French emperor, who was not averse to a change of the *status quo*. It was during those few years of what appeared to be French primacy that the new states of Germany and Italy appeared. As A. J. P. Taylor has expressed this point, 'If Russia was indeed the tyrant of Europe, then the Crimean war was a war of liberation. This liberation delivered Europe first into the hands of Napoleon III then into those of Bismarck.'[6]

So the revision of the 1815 settlement that occurred after the middle of the nineteenth century can be explained in terms of the changing pattern in the distribution of power between those states dedicated to the preservation of the *status quo* and those prepared to accept change. But by saying that after the Crimean war, European international politics returned to the balance-of-power system, more is intended than that there was a change in the distribution of power. What is being referred to is the new-found autonomy of the states within the European system, the increasing feeling that the destiny of each state lay in her own hands, not in a European Concert, that a state's interests could best be achieved by reliance on her own efforts and energies rather than by reliance on international procedures. The most evident sign that such a change was in fact taking place is, as Hinsley has argued, the return to precise and offensive military alliances, the primary purpose of which was to secure the neutrality or the assistance of another power in a projected war, alliances that characterised the period 1859–71 – in other words, a return to the type of alliance that had been characteristic of the eighteenth century but had been unheard of in the period 1815–58. And again, that the powers should have returned to such alliance systems *after* 1870, can largely be explained by the success of such alliances and understandings during the wars that produced Italy and Germany. In these various pacts and alliances you can see a quite radical departure from the international-conference approach of the first half of the century to an approach based quite explicitly on unilateral redistribution of territories and on the engineering of favourable international alignments in order to secure such redistributions. In other words, the ultimate sanction of a territorial change was no longer the voice of the Concert of Europe but rather whether or not there existed a margin of power sufficiently large to enforce such a redistribution.

The lessons learned by the European statesmen from the experience of the 1850s and 1860s, during which the new states of Italy and Germany made their appearance, were not lost on the post-1870 period. There was, however, to be one important change. The alliances after 1870 were without exception defensive whereas the earlier ones had been offensive. But this change should not blind us to a fundamental point of similarity –

which was that the powers still thought that their interests could best be enhanced by bilateral or trilateral alliances rather than by Europe acting in concert. That there was a change from the offensive alliance to the defensive can, in fact, be readily explained by the changed nature of the post-1870 situation. If until the achievement of a German state, Bismarck had been essentially revisionist as far as the European settlement was concerned, after 1870 his diplomacy was aimed at preservation of the newly established *status quo*. The defensive alliance was a device appropriate to this more conservative period.

It requires no special insight to realise that balance-of-power principles underlay most of the provisions of these alliances of the last quarter of the century. The entire alliance structures of the period centred on Berlin. Bismarck's fundamental objective was to secure agreements with both Austria and Russia. One was necessary with Austria because their interests seemed to overlap, as both Germany and Austria were central European powers. He needed an alliance with Russia for two reasons. One was to act as a restraining influence on both Russia and Austria and so prevent a clash of these powers in the Balkans. More importantly, if Russia was ignored by Berlin, the chances were that the Austro-German alliance would produce a counterweight in the shape of some agreement between Russia and France. It was to prevent such an eventuality that Bismarck signed his Reinsurance Treaty with Russia. This treaty lapsed in 1890, the year in which Bismarck was dismissed from office and his successor did not believe in taking the same precautions. Within a year or two, Russia and France had entered into negotiations which produced their alliance of 1894, thus presenting Germany with the nightmare which Bismarck had sought to prevent – that of a potential war on two fronts. Europe had therefore split up into two camps: Germany, Austria and Italy, on the one hand, and Russia and France on the other. Britain remained aloof from either grouping. In every sense, this was the classical balance-of-power situation.

It was an age dominated by balance-of-power considerations in yet another sense and this was in the relationship between Europe and the outside world. There are various aspects of this inter-relationship that deserve attention: European sources of the

imperialist expansion of the powers; extra-European developments as a limiting factor on diplomacy within Europe; and the
changing status of Europe as a whole within the global framework. In each aspect, the powers were motivated essentially by
calculations deriving from balance-of-power principles rather
than from concern with a Concert of Europe.

Most strikingly there was the general European expansion into
Africa and Asia in the last quarter of the nineteenth century. It
has been the contention of many historians that this development can be adequately explained by reference to the internal
balance of the European state system. It is a common characteristic of such explanations that they emphasise the importance of
the 'official mind of imperialism' – that is, they see the European
governments as positive actors not, as Hobson and Lenin would
have it, as mere tools in the hands of some sectional or class
interest. Moreover, the European governments, according to this
perspective, calculated almost exclusively in terms of national
strategy – of preserving or destroying the particular balance that
existed between the European powers.

A few examples would help to illustrate this approach. If we
look at the international situation in Europe in the last two
decades of the nineteenth century, it can be argued that the
alignment of the powers was becoming decreasingly flexible and
that any attempt to alter the balance in Europe by tampering
with the political map of Europe itself could have resulted in a
general war. Given this stalemate in Europe, the powers played
out their game in Africa and Asia. The classic demonstration of
this relationship is perhaps to be found in the partition of Africa.
According to this interpretation, the partition was sparked by the
somewhat fortuitous British occupation of Egypt in 1882, the
consequences of which were to be felt throughout the length of
the continent as the powers bartered and bargained for their
shares in the territorial carve-up in which, in addition to Britain,
the countries of France, Germany, Italy, Portugal and Belgium
were the main participants.

The reason why Germany entered the race for colonial pos-
sessions has been explained in terms of this balance syndrome.
While it has often been argued that throughout the nineteenth
century, Britain, by pursuing a policy of splendid isolation perfor-

med the role of the balancer in the European system, from another perspective it can be seen that Britain, far from being a balancing or stabilising element in the situation, was in fact the main destabilising factor. One theorist of balance-of-power systems, Morton Kaplan, has stated the proposition that 'a condition which makes unstable the balance of power system is the existence of an essential national actor who does not play according to the rules of the game, the existence of a national actor whose essential national goals are oriented towards the establishment of some form of supranational political organisation'. Just such an actor was Britain. Clearly, while Britain was not creating a supra-national political organisation in the sense of a hegemonic empire within Europe, outside Europe the extent of the British Empire represented a gross imbalance that no other power could rival. It was in order to rectify this balance that Germany, too, sought her place in the sun.

On the other hand, it was a German move in China that was to precipitate in 1898 the scramble for concessions in that country. Germany secured a lease of a Chinese port and within the year Russia, Britain and France had secured similar concessions. Lord Salisbury the British Prime Minister justified the British acquisition of the lease of Wei hai wei as a response to the Russian lease of Port Arthur, which, he said, 'had materially altered the balance of power'.

That the colonial expansion of the period was related to the European balance, but in the reverse direction, is also suggested by the nature of Anglo-Russian rivalry in Central Asia throughout the nineteenth century. The British in India, in pursuit of their forward policy, had continually pushed outward the north-west frontier, even fighting wars in Afghanistan to counter what was believed to be a Russian threat to India. Simultaneously, the Tsar of Russia had in the course of the 1850s and 1860s enclosed vast areas of Central Asia within the Russian Empire. By the end of the century, the two empires were separated only by a grey area, Persia and Afghanistan, in which the two empires vied with each other to secure political or economic control. In 1907, however, Britain and Russia signed their 'entente', calling a truce in their rivalry in Persia. And it is obvious that their reason for doing so was their common need to contain Germany within

Europe. In other words, the imperial expansion of Europe in Asia was not only inspired by the dictates of the European balance but it was also limited by such considerations. After a century of rivalry in Asia, Britain and Russia came to terms when they realised that their common fear of Germany was stronger than their mutual fears of each other.

The third element in this inter-relationship is the decreasing stature of Europe in relation to other emerging Great Powers on the international scene, or, to express the same point slightly differently, the extension or globalisation of the European balance system.

Basically the thesis is as follows, as one writer has expressed it.

As the German attempts in 1914 and 1939 to break through into the ranks of the world powers were to show, Bismarck had created a state sufficiently strong not only to dominate Europe but also to challenge and compete on terms of near-equality with the great extra-European powers ... from about 1890, the overhauling of Europe by Russia and America ... was resumed and intensified. Although its victories in 1870 and its rapid industrialisation had raised Germany to a new eminence, it was also, in view of the rising power of the United States and Russia, in a precarious position in the longer term, aware of its great potentialities but aware also that it had a definite time limit within which to exploit its superiority; and this fact imparted an ebullient quality to German policy from the accession of William II in 1888 to the days of Hitler.[7]

In other words, the German attempts to establish hegemony in 1914 and 1939 were more than repeat examples of the numerous historical instances of attempts to achieve preponderance within Europe – they were more than the linear descendants of the exploits of Louis XIV and of Napoleon. In what way did they differ? They differed in that for Germany, in the two world wars, the acquisition of European hegemony was but a stepping-stone to playing an influential role in a future system dominated by large global empires – Britain, Russia, America and, she hoped, Germany. This is the underlying thesis of Fritz Fischer's controversial book on Germany's war aims in the First World War,[8] where Fischer seeks to establish that Germany's leaders were influenced by such ideas and sought to create an empire based on Europe and Africa because they saw the future no longer in terms of the old European system of states but in terms of a new system of world states.

In less grandiose terms, there is an obvious sense in which extra-European powers were being called upon to function as adjuncts of a European system that was no longer, as hitherto, sufficient unto itself. This was to be demonstrated most palpably by the American intervention in the 1914–18 war but there were harbingers of this trend in existence before the outbreak of the Great War. Notably, in 1902, Britain called upon the services of Japan to consolidate the former's global position because of the increasing difficulty experienced by Britain of serving as counterpoise to Germany within Europe while also pursuing imperial objectives in the Far East. As has been said elsewhere of the Anglo-Japanese alliance, 'a member of the inner circle of European great powers was calling on an Asian state to join the international system in order to redress an imbalance of power at the core of that system'.[9]

It would be inappropriate at this stage to consider in a serious fashion the origins of the First World War. However, as we are interested in the dominant traits of international political behaviour of this period, a few comments on the relationship between that behaviour and the outbreak of war may be apposite.

The first notion that we should disabuse ourselves of is that the war flowed inevitably from the alliances we have been discussing. There is a tendency, having described the European alignments of the 1880s and 1890s – Germany, Italy and Austria against Russia and France – to read them forward into 1914 and to cite them as the main cause of the war. While this is not entirely without foundation, it suggests a view of international history which is too superficial. The opposing alliances were in no sense rigid unshakeable blocs. The Moroccan crises of 1905 and 1911 and the various Balkan crises of the pre-war period showed that there was sufficient flexibility within these alliances if the statesmen wanted to make use of it. Of these original alliance systems, Italy of course was to defect from the Austro-German camp. And even after the signing of the Anglo-French and Anglo-Russian ententes, there was no guarantee that Britain would enter any war on the side of France and Russia. Indeed, it seems clear that German calculations were predicated on a belief that Britain would remain neutral, a belief that Britain did little to shake.

Far from the alliances presenting rigid blocs, there are numerous examples of contacts and negotiations cutting across these
alignments. On occasions, France and Germany made common
cause in Africa against Britain. Likewise, albeit for her own ends,
Germany encouraged, and to some extent was an accomplice of,
Russian involvement in the Far East. There were also several
attempts, especially in the 1898–1901 period, to start serious
negotiations between Germany and Britain because in many
ways British and German interests conflicted less seriously than
did those of Britain on the one hand, and France and Russia on
the other.

As yet another example of the lack of rigidity of the alliances, it
has been argued that the Franco-Russian alliance of 1894 was
intended not to cement a new European alignment but to restore
an old one, in that both states were looking to the past rather
than to the future. As A. J. P. Taylor has contended 'each power
was still looking over its shoulder. The Russians hoped that the
entente would lead Germany to renew the Reinsurance Treaty,
the French that it would lead Great Britain to compromise in the
Egyptian question.'[10]

Certainly, the alliances did divide Europe into the two camps
that were to fight the war. But it would be too simplistic to
accuse Bismarck of causing the First World War.

Perhaps more important than the Austro-German alliance
itself was the particular turn that Austro-German relations took
in 1906. The German chief of staff, Schlieffen, who had drawn up
a German war plan, in the event of a war on two fronts, had
thereby antagonised Austria, first by refusing to co-ordinate plans
with her and, secondly, because his plan of military operations
concentrated on the west and then on the east. That is to say that
Schlieffen's plan was for a quick knock-out blow against France
after which German troops would be transferred to the eastern
front. But given that Austria's collision was likely to be with
Russia, this scarcely met the order of Austrian priorities – just as,
in 1944, the allies' decision to open a second front in France
scarcely met with the order of Soviet priorities. Anyway,
Schlieffen's successor, Moltke, set out in 1906 to repair the
damage with Austria and did so by making new commitments to
Austria in order to convince her of Germany's good faith. By

1909 there is evidence that Moltke was practically admitting to Austria that Germany would back her even in a war caused by Austria's own provocation. Unfortunately, as various analysts have pointed out, at the very moment that he was making commitments to Austria that increased the likelihood of war with Russia, Moltke insisted that the war must be fought in accordance with Schlieffen's prescription – that is, that it must start with a German attack on France. In their insistence upon fighting the war in this way, the military chiefs had ensured that Germany took the initiative in declaring war on Russia and France and that she invaded Belgium. In other words, Germany put beyond question the fact that an Austro-Russian war would be a European war.

Another way of looking at the First World War is to approach it from the perspective of the long-term interests of Russia and Austria in the Balkans that were to provide the immediate occasion for the war. To a certain extent, Europe had preserved the peace by channelling off its inner tensions into overseas expansion. With the first decade of the twentieth century, however, Europe began once again to turn in upon itself. This indicated that the Balkans would be the most likely scene of conflict.

Austria had seen her options as to possible spheres of influence steadily foreclosed. The war against Cavour and Napoleon in 1859 had served notice that Italy would no longer be Austria's own little preserve and with the achievement of Italian unification, Austria was largely excluded from expansion in a southwesterly direction. The same was to happen in the north. Her defeat by Prussia in 1866 was a signal that Austria would no longer be the preponderant power in Germany. The smaller states of Germany now fell under the sway of Prussia. So again, an Austrian sphere of influence in the north had been foreclosed as an option. All that remained was expansion in the direction of the south-east, towards the Balkans, and it was in this direction that Austria was steadily attracted throughout the late nineteenth and early twentieth centuries.

All would have been well had Russia not made the same decision at the same time. Russian interest in the eastern question and in securing parts of the disintegrating Ottoman Empire dates back at least to the eighteenth century. However, for the last

quarter of the nineteenth century, after having her fingers slightly burned at the Congress of Berlin, which ended the Balkan crisis of 1877–8, Russia temporarily shifted the focus of her interest away from this area, which was proving too dangerous. She found the atmosphere for expansion more congenial in Central Asia and in the Far East. However, developments in Europe led Britain and Russia to sign a truce on the Central Asian question in 1907. And similarly, Russia's humiliating defeat at the hands of Japan, in 1904, foreclosed the Far East as a possible area for Russian expansion at this time. Like Austria, Russia found that her energies were coming increasingly to be devoted to the Balkan region. In the end, this was to spell disaster.

The specific question of culpability need not detain us here. There is an obvious sense in which Germany's potential strength was disruptive of the European equilibrium but we should be hesitant in proceeding to adduce culpability from this fact alone. It is a perennial feature of international history, and of the structure of conflicts more generally, that the rising power – or the anti-*status-quo* party, must seem to be the 'aggressor' state or the 'disruptive' element: such is an inevitable accompaniment of the cyclical rise and fall of states. In consequence, as Germany sought to find her place in an international order in which Britain had hitherto been *primus inter pares*, the appearance was created that Germany's *Weltpolitik* was undermining the stability of the system. However, unless the pre-existing order had some special legitimacy associated with it, it is difficult to see how the intrusion of Germany into that structure makes her, in any meaningful sense, culpable.

There may well be a parallel between Germany's challenge to the Pax Britannica at the turn of the century and the Soviet challenge, from the 1960s onwards, to the Pax Americana. In this latter case, it was the Soviet Union who was the late arrival in terms of global military capacity and in that sense, it must appear that the Soviet attempt to secure her 'place in the sun' is 'destabilising' and 'threatening'. This is, however, no more than to say that the 'first comer' stands in possession of rights that the aspirant must later challenge and from this perspective it would seem misleading to confuse a moral situation – culpability – with a chronological one – change.

It has been the argument of this chapter that international

politics in the 1856–1914 period were – in contrast to the years 1815–54 – characterised by balance-of-power mechanisms rather than by Concert procedures. The real problem lies in trying to explain why this should have been so. In this context, the immediate dilemma emanates from our inability to disentangle the alliances as the *source* of the heightened insecurity of the pre-war generation – and thus as the factor that lent the period its characteristic mood – from the alliances as a *symptom* of insecurity and therefore as a mere reflection of more profound processes at work. Just as we earlier pondered whether the Concert created the peace or simply mirrored it, we are now bemused by the alternatives as to whether it was balance tactics that created the tension, or the tension that dictated the tactics.

Presumably, the relationship is symbiotic, which is a trivial observation, but from it we might make the more important deduction that 'moods' of international politics, and the characteristic modes of statecraft associated with them, tend to be, in the short term, self-reinforcing. Expectations of a Concert approach to international problems tend to produce conditions in which a Concert can function with some degree of success: alternatively, expectations of a purely competitive approach tend to ensure that this is the least, and the most, that the system will be able to aspire to.

One last point needs to be made. If the Concert of Europe fused the elements of Great-Power tutelage and of international diplomatic machinery, the period 1856–1914 witnessed once again the bifurcation of these two themes of modern international history. A balance-of-power system is, *de facto*, one in which the major powers have special rights and privileges, and what is interesting about this period, as compared with the earlier part of the century, is that there was little attempt to introduce additional diplomatic norms or conventions over and above the basic rules that a balance system itself prescribes.

This does not mean that the later nineteenth century was devoid of efforts to ameliorate the practices by means of which states conducted their diplomacy: the attempts to institute some form of arbitration apparatus, which was perhaps the characteristic avenue of exploration of the age, would belie such a statement. Nevertheless, these efforts were little more than a faint

descant in a diplomatic melody dominated by another mood. While it makes some kind of sense to regard the Concert as a fusion of 'utopian' and 'realist' elements, in the latter half of the century the utopian pursuit of peace is a story of its own, wholly divorced from the manner in which the powers went about their daily task of creating international order.

6 *Concert without balance: 1918–1939*

In grossly simplified terms, we might describe the historical periods so far considered in the following terms. From 1815 to 1854 there was a stable distribution of power upon which the powers were able to base a successful Concert; whereas from 1856 to 1914, while there may well have been periods of equilibrium, the powers were unable to operate a system in which Concert principles played any significant part. From this perspective, the period 1919–39 represents a third distinctive form of 'international order' in the sense that its dominant feature was an attempt to operate a highly formalised and institutionalised Concert system, namely the League of Nations, but that, as there was a fundamental disequilibrium within the system, the conditions for Concert were not present and the actual practice of states bore little resemblance to the Concert principles formally enshrined in the League. In other words, the 1919–39 period may be viewed as having characteristics of both these former ages: like 1815–54 there was a collectivist aspiration and an attempt to introduce new diplomatic norms; like 1856–1914 the powers were thrown back upon their own individual resources and reverted, almost without exception, to traditional balance devices. We might say that as far as the 'heart' was concerned, the inter-war years shared the sentiments of Concert diplomacy whilst the 'head' dictated a continuance of late-nineteenth-century balance strategies.

The First World War and the settlement that ended it were to have a profound influence on subsequent international relations. Perhaps most obviously, the Versailles treaty defined the structure of international politics in the inter-war period. The war saw the destruction of Europe's three major empires, the Russian, the Austro-Hungarian and the German. In place of the former Austro-Hungarian Empire, Europe saw the rebirth of several successor states, which greatly complicated the map of the continent. It was in the context of this new territorial distribution

that international politics were to be conducted during the next two decades.

However, the consequences of the war were to be more far-reaching than this. In fact, it can be argued that many of the developments that are normally associated with the post-1945 period can more properly be seen to have had their origins in the war of 1914–18 and its immediate aftermath. This point can be made with reference to several aspects of contemporary international relations.

It is often claimed that one of the most salient characteristics of the post-1945 period has been the revolution in military technology. This in turn is said to have resulted in a pronounced decline in the utility of military force. Without minimising the impact of nuclear weapons on current strategic thought and on the political uses of war, there is some validity in the view that, if war can no longer be regarded as a useful instrument of political persuasion, then the trend towards this point of view was already well established by 1918. The basic argument as it applies to nuclear weapons is that the consequences of nuclear war would far outweigh any possible benefits resulting from the war and that therefore military force is obsolete. Although the scale of magnitude is perhaps different, the First World War led to exactly the same conclusions. Whereas the wars of the nineteenth century, namely those of Bismarck, had been short and efficient, the 1914–18 war, in terms of its territorial stagnation and its unprecedented loss of life, was to cast serious doubts on the efficacy of military power and on its appropriateness for settling political disputes.

A second revolution that is generally thought to have been triggered off by the Second World War is the independence movement in the Afro-Asian countries. But again, while as a matter of strict historical detail this is true, there seems to be at least some reason for arguing that several liberation movements were given a major stimulus by the First World War. The principle of national self-determination was given limited sanction in Eastern Europe and this in itself pointed to the contradictions in maintaining colonial rule outside Europe. To express the point in a wide historical perspective, if the movement

for independence in the colonial territories was, in a sense, merely the obverse side of the decline of Europe and of the decline of the imperial powers, then this decline, although concealed during the inter-war period, certainly dates from the First World War rather than from the Second.

The First World War was to lead directly to another revolutionary transformation in world politics. This was of course the Russian Revolution of 1917. And this suggests another way in which it is possible to argue that the historical creator of the present framework of international relations was the 1914–18 period rather than the aftermath of 1945. This is that both the power-political and the ideological bases of Soviet–American hostility originated in the immediate revolutionary aftermath. The ideological Cold War had its roots in the opposing conceptions of international order put forward by Lenin and by President Wilson: the power-political antagonism between the two states had its origins in direct American military intervention against the Soviet regime during the civil war within Russia. As Mayer has pointed out, one of the most momentous developments of the war was the simultaneous emergence of Washington and Petrograd as two rival centres of power, both of which momentarily abandoned the old diplomacy.[1] On the Soviet side, the Bolsheviks renounced the former Russian imperial objectives, especially Russian designs on Constantinople, and they published the secret wartime treaties signed with the allies. On the American side, Woodrow Wilson, too, came out against the old diplomacy and advocated its replacement by open treaties openly arrived at. This conflict between the old and the new diplomacy was to have important consequences for future international relations. It postulated two radically different conceptions of foreign-policy formulation. On the one hand, the old diplomacy clung to the idea that foreign policy was best made by professional diplomats behind closed doors and immune from national politics. As against this, the advocates of the new diplomacy argued that such a method had resulted in the 1914–18 war. To remedy this situation, foreign policy should be opened to the influence of public opinion. The argument held that just as increased democratisation of domestic politics had produced important economic and social reforms, so the foreign policies of

democratic states could also improve as a result of popular participation and control. In effect, the contention was that, unlike the officials of the foreign offices, the public at large would not tolerate aggressive policies. Stimulated by the Russian Revolution on the one side and President Wilson on the other, these ideas increased in influence during 1917–18 and began to have a powerful effect on the war aims of the allies, culminating in the apparent allied acceptance of Wilson's fourteen points as the basis for a post-war settlement. Most obviously, also, the 1914–18 war gave birth to the League of Nations, which concerns us because, as one historian has expressed it, 'for the first time in history an attempt was made to formalize in law the organization of international order'.[2]

Historically, the lineage of the League may be divided into three periods: first, an evolution from, and a reaction against, international practice in the nineteenth century; secondly, the experiences of the 1914–18 war itself; and thirdly, the particular international configuration that prevailed at the end of the war and provided the environment in which the Versailles treaty was signed and the League was set up.

Intellectually, the origins of the League were manifold. It is possible to trace back a strand of intellectual speculation about the problems of achieving peace almost to the beginning of the European state system itself. Although the various peace projects of the sixteenth, seventeenth and eighteenth centuries were in no sense direct precursors of the League of Nations, they do contain a rich body of philosophical writings that is very much relevant to the problems of maintaining peace between independent states and relevant also to the philosophical basis of any international organisation. It is also possible to distinguish the influence of mid-nineteenth-century liberalism, of the peace movement of the second half of the century, of international socialism, of the various peace societies that sprang up – especially in Britain and the United States – during the war years, and, unmistakeably, the emerging Wilsonian ethos of international relations. However, if the intellectual origins of the League were partly the product of evolution, they were also partly the product of a revolution caused by the psychological crisis of the war.

The League was in a very specific sense a reaction to the

World War of 1914–18. It must be remembered that with the exception of the few clinical wars of German and Italian unification in the middle of the century, the European powers had enjoyed almost a century of peace. That is not to say that there were not many crises during the period and perhaps an unprecedented degree of rivalry and conflict between the powers outside of Europe. But at the same time, the 1914–18 war did come as a psychological shock to a generation brought up to think of peace as being the normal state of affairs. Additionally, while the few wars of the nineteenth century had been of short duration, the 1914–18 war, which many thought would be over by Christmas of 1914, continued until 1918 with casualties at quite unprecedented levels. It is small wonder that such a war had a powerful and revolutionary effect on statesmen at the time. As has been said

> The Great War ... by its destructiveness, by its overthrow of all that had been regarded as stable in international politics, compelled men to seek for new and surer forms of organisation. And at the same time, by the associated effort which the war called out for its own purposes, it provided working models for the peace time machinery of the future.[3]

Indeed, when we recall the extent of co-operation in the prosecution of the war, we might accept the verdict that 'the League to come was hardly a step forward. It was a measure of demobilisation in international organisation'.[4]

If the League was a reaction to the war in general, it was also more specifically a reaction to the international conditions that were believed to have brought it about. Statesmen picked out what they considered to be the main features of international life in the pre-war era and calculated that by changing these features peace would be ensured. No one expressed this point of view more vocally than the American President, Woodrow Wilson. Wilson's particular target was what may be called the morality of the old European diplomacy. If it is true that Americans in general shared a distaste for the methods and practices of European statecraft, Wilson was particularly obsessed with this great evil. It was a sentiment that he was often to repeat.

> It is plain that this war could have come only as it did, suddenly out of secret counsels without warning to the world ... And the lesson which the shock of being taken by surprise in a matter so deeply vital to all the

nations of the world has made poignantly clear is that the peace of the world must henceforth depend upon a new and more wholesome diplomacy.[5]

It was a view that saw war as the product of the unscrupulous machinations of diplomats.

It is now time to turn to a more detailed analysis of the ideas and practices underlying the League itself. It must be remembered that the League was engaged in a whole range of managerial functions – dealing with economic issues, communications, transport, health etc. There was also the International Labour Organisation. And one other function should be referred to: the mandate system – the arrangement devised by the League for the supervision of the colonial territories of the defeated powers. However, while all these functions were important, the following observations are confined to the central issue – that of the League as a peace-keeping institution.

Broadly speaking, the League of Nations may be regarded as a synthesis of three devices that had only partially been realised in the international diplomacy of the nineteenth and early twentieth centuries. These were:

(1) a permanent apparatus for regular conferences;
(2) a system of arbitration directed by a permanent judicial organ;
(3) a system of guarantees.

The precise nature of the conference system established by the League is illustrative of the influence of the nineteenth century and of the felt need to improve on that earlier system. Basic features of the League approach were its permanent framework, its regularity of meetings and its approach towards universality. The Bismarckian wars had revealed the speed with which an attack could be launched in the age of the railway and in consequence the procedure for the summoning of conferences was in need of lubrication if a peace-keeping function was to be performed. Hence the need for a secretariat and fixed procedural rules. Again, while conferences were a fairly typical means of diplomacy during the nineteenth century, they were sporadic rather than regular – in the words of one historian, 'the medicine of Europe rather than its daily bread'.[6] Thus, the Concert of Europe ceased to function if the national interest of one of the

powers required it to have a free hand: conferences disappeared from the international scene during the wars of Italian and German unification. No conference was summoned in 1914. The shortcomings of such a system, the League sought to rectify by regularising the meetings of the Assembly and of the Council.

The structure of the League itself reflects an unhappy balance between two conceptions of its membership, a conflict produced by the historical development of the conference system. The nineteenth-century Concert was composed essentially of the Great Powers. The reluctance of the powers to share their dominant position in the system was bolstered by wartime experience: if military co-operation during the 1914–18 war proved to be useful experience for future international organisation, it also strengthened the conception of the allies as the directors and executors of the international system, an attitude scarcely concealed at the Versailles conference. However, this elite ethos amongst the powers came into direct conflict with the Wilsonian ideal of self-determination and with any attempt to base the new international system on the moral force of world opinion. Hence the Council, originally envisaged as the organ of the victorious powers, was diluted by the inclusion of some of the smaller states and the Assembly gained some status as against the Council.

Implicit in this ideal of a permanent framework for discussion is the notion of open diplomacy. The preamble to the convenant required 'open, just and honourable' relations between nations, and Article 18 required all treaties to be registered with the League. It is not difficult to see in this the aversion from the alliance diplomacy of the pre-war generation and the high place that secret diplomacy was accorded in the assessments of the causes of tension leading to the war. Also, if Wilson's vision of the League as the tribunal of world opinion was to become operative such openness would be necessary: instigation of the international 'hue and cry' presupposed knowledge of developments in the system that were contrary to the ideals of the League.

A second major element in the League complex was the apparatus of conciliation described in the convenant. The dual nature of this instrument reflected the two strands of its historical evolution. On the one hand there was to be the process of judicial arbitration by means of the Permanent Court of International

Justice. Such a judicial organ had been striven for at the Hague conferences but they merely succeeded in establishing what has been described as a permanent framework for *ad hoc* tribunals.[7]

Disputes not submitted to judicial arbitration were to be presented to the Council, which had to endeavour to effect a settlement of the dispute. In this provision can be distinguished a lineage going back to the congress system and existing in a weaker form in the Concert of Europe whereby the major powers took it upon themselves to preserve the peace of Europe. However, such a blatant form of power politics was considered unacceptable by the exponents of the new diplomacy. The remains of a Great-Power directorship of the European peace lingered on, however, in the League Council with the qualification, as Inis Claude has expressed it, that if the Council was a new edition of the Concert of Europe, it was at least a significantly revised edition.[8]

The third essential element incorporated in the League of Nations was a system of guarantees. The guarantee was no innovation of the twentieth century: the most notable example of a guarantee in the nineteenth century, the relevance of which was highlighted in 1914, was that accorded to Belgium by the powers. It was also an instrument well known on the other side of the Atlantic, the home of the Monroe doctrine. It can be argued, however, that the guarantee embodied in the convenant was given a subtle twist by the particular condition of the international situation at the end of the war in as much as the essence of the guarantee was the preservation of the *status quo post bellum*. Thus, it has been said that 'the function envisaged for the League was ... to legitimise and stabilise a particular world settlement based upon victory'.[9] In so far as this is true, it is reminiscent of the purposes of the congress system following upon the 1815 Vienna settlement.

The point about this view is that it brings an important perspective to the study of the League of Nations. There is a temptation to regard the League as the almost inevitable outcome of the precedents, organisational precursors and theoretical frameworks of the nineteenth century. As a corrective to this, it is important to stress the view of the League, implicit in the description of it as the stabiliser of the post-war situation, as the

particular response to a particular historical situation. This view emphasises the role of such immediate factors as wartime experience, the particular condition of world opinion and the particular energies of the societies and personalities whose ideas helped to shape the covenant. Above all, it should be remembered that the covenant was no sacred document, delivered from on high, like the ten commandments. It was very much a political document and as such was a compromise between the various views of security held by the major powers.

How are we to assess the nature of the League, given the attitude with which the powers approached it and the general spirit surrounding the post-war settlement as a whole? In this context, it is difficult to avoid the conclusion that the League was a veneer underneath which traditional policies were pursued. Such a case can be made against America. Once you cut away the rhetoric surrounding the American intervention in the First World War, one is left with the harsh reality that America became involved because it would have been contrary to her interests to have had Europe dominated by an expansionist German state. If the American decision to join the war effort did not come until 1917, it is nonetheless significant that it came at a point when Germany was probably closer to victory than at any other stage of the war. If we consider Europe in terms of the traditional balance-of-power system, it looks very much as if America was entering the game to take the place of one of the former players, Russia, who was temporarily unable to play her role. Unfortunately, being an inexperienced player, America had no deep understanding of the game. Having thrown her weight into the balance at the crucial moment in order to prevent German predominance, America then reverted immediately to continental isolation. She seemed to believe that the balance once restored would remain in equilibrium. She failed to understand the simple point that just as her intervention had restored the European balance in 1918, so her refusal to play a permanent role in Europe was to leave the door open to a further challenge to this balance.

France, to sketch out an argument that will be developed in detail below, was obsessed by fears for her own security and saw the League and the Versailles settlement solely in these terms. In

a sense, French statesmen were more realistic than their Anglo-Saxon counterparts. They realised that the post-war settlement rested on an elaborate fiction. The fiction was that France, after 1919, was the most powerful state in Europe. This was a fiction because the conditions that led to this situation were wholly artificial. They rested on the artificial constraint of Germany through the Versailles provisions. They rested on the fact that these conditions had been imposed on Germany, not by French power alone but additionally by British and American power. They rested on the temporary exclusion of the Soviet Union from the European scene in the aftermath of the revolution. Probably the French themselves appreciated the artificial nature of the post-war structure better than anyone. That is why they demanded that traditional balance-of-power considerations should be included in the settlement.

Realising that the post-war situation was artificial but realising also that France's security depended on this artificial situation being preserved, France saw the main function of the League of Nations as being the maintenance of the territorial *status quo* established at Versailles. Any form of change could only make this artificial situation less favourable to France. But already there were signs that this fiction could not persist. If France's position depended on being underwritten by Britain and America, then unfortunately these two countries soon made it clear that they would not underwrite the European settlement. America did not ratify the covenant and so did not join the League of Nations.

If the Versailles settlement was all along the embodiment of traditional power-objectives on the part of the European states, then this rubbed off on the League of Nations, which came to appear as the instrument for maintaining this settlement. The reason for this was that the League covenant was written into the peace treaties themselves. Even more importantly, the League was an instrument in the hands of the victors and in the hands of those victors most dedicated to security through traditional balance practices. America, from which the original idealistic impulse had come, as we have seen, did not become a member of the League. Germany was not to be permitted to join until she had demonstrated, through her adherence to the dis-

armament and reparations clauses of the settlement, that she was fit to be a member of such an international organisation. And Russia and the League viewed each other with mutual distrust and hostility. In short, the League as an international instrument fell into the hands of France and Britain. Britain, feeling that because of her navy many of the duties of League enforcement would fall upon her and being reluctant to undertake these duties, was slightly embarrassed by the League and sought to play it down. France, meanwhile, saw it as the only means of preserving the European *status quo* upon which she thought her security depended. If this was the Concert, then it was indeed a Concert of the most minimal kind.

From what has been said so far, it is clear that the League failed to establish itself as an organisation capable of rising above the individual national interests of the principal member states. It is this fact which forms the basis of E. H. Carr's critique of the League and of the Versailles settlement.[10] The point emerges repeatedly in Carr's discussion of the inter-war period. As he said at one point, with respect to the collective security principles of the League, 'these supposedly absolute and universal principles were not principles at all, but the unconscious reflections of national policy based on a particular interpretation of national interest at a particular time'.[11] In other words what was described as collective security was little other than the placing of predominant power in the hands of the victor states and thus ensuring that there could be no challenge to the *status quo*. If we accept this point of view, then it leads to the conclusion that the failure of the League of Nations was not so much the failure of collective security as the failure of those powers entrusted with the monopoly of power in the post-war situation to maintain their monopoly of that power. To quote again from E. H. Carr, who makes a similar point very well, 'it is necessary to dispel the illusion that the policy of these states which are broadly speaking satisfied with the status quo and whose watchword is security is somehow less concerned with power than the policy of the dissatisfied states'.[12] In other words, the League did not banish power considerations from international politics only to see them revived in the form of renewed Japanese, Italian and German expansion. Rather, power was basic to the very formation of the

League. If a change did occur from the 1920s to the 1930s then it was not a change to power politics; rather it was a change with respect to which states were using the power – from the *status quo* to the revisionist states.

It may be appropriate at this stage to draw attention to some of the striking parallels and some of the striking differences between the settlement of 1815 and that of 1919. Both settlements had been necessitated by the need to repair a European continent severely disrupted by long and protracted war. Both witnessed important redrawings of the map of Europe in accordance with political and strategic requirements of security. But while both settlements redrew the map of Europe in accordance with traditional security dictates, at the same time both settlements gave expression to a reaction against the diplomacy that had caused the preceding war. The 1815 settlement gave birth to the congress system whilst the 1919 settlement gave birth to the League of Nations. Both were important experiments in reordering the basic techniques for the management of international relations.

While there are these similarities between the two settlements, there is at least one important contrast: that whereas the Vienna settlement was to last, with the exception of the revisions executed in the middle of the century, until 1914, the 1919 settlement did not last two decades. This has led one historian to observe, rather cynically, that in 1815 the framers of the settlement dealt with questions of power and preserved the peace for a century whilst in 1919 statesmen dealt with questions of justice and morality and kept the peace for less than twenty years. This comment is slightly misguided. As we have seen, the 1919 settlement in the final analysis was little more concerned with questions of justice and morality than that of 1815. In fact, the primary considerations, international security and opposition to internal revolution, were largely the same both in 1815 and 1919.

So what, then, explains the apparent success of the Vienna settlement and the apparent failure of the Versailles settlement? There are probably several explanations that could be put forward but only one will be mentioned: and that was that whereas the 1815 peace left no major dissatisfied power, France having been reinstated as a full member of the international club, the 1919 settlement was considered by one major power,

Germany, to be intolerable and from the very beginning there were appeals for revision of the treaty. How, in turn, you would explain this is another and an extremely difficult question. The following argument is largely an extension of that put forward by Mayer:[13] it hinges on the role of public opinion in the framing of the settlement. Perhaps, in 1815, the professional diplomats had greater freedom to draw up a treaty that was based solely on considerations of balance and security without the intrusion of popular demands for revenge and for the imposition of punitive conditions on the vanquished. It has been said of the Vienna settlement that it was negotiated 'in elegant and ceremonious privacy'.[14] This was not the case in 1919 when a whole host of internal considerations impinged on the calculations of the peacemakers. If this appears too simple an explanation, then perhaps we should try to explain why a war-guilt clause was imposed on Germany in 1919 but no such document on France in 1815, and it seems that one reason for this is that such emotional gestures are designed for the consumption of public opinion. However, the emotional reaction against the war-guilt clause was to play a large part in the undermining of the entire Versailles settlement. Perhaps, then, it is not too superficial to explain the relative successes of the two settlements in terms of the ages that produced them – the age of aristocratic politics on the one hand and the age of emerging mass politics on the other.

Thus far we have discussed the general atmosphere surrounding the Versailles settlement and the inception of the League. How are we now to analyse the pattern of international order that emerged and developed during the inter-war years? It will be the argument of the remainder of this chapter that the postwar settlement was based on certain false assumptions, already alluded to in passing, and that these assumptions led to a 'schizophrenic' international order in which the policies of the powers were pursued at two quite distinct levels. At the one level, the powers participated in an elaborate myth. At the more profound level, the powers were very consciously aware of the underlying reality of the situation. The description of the inter-war period is, then, that during the 1920s the myth and the reality managed to coexist with each other whereas in the 1930s the myth was destroyed and only the reality remained.

What then were the elements of the myth that permeated the international politics of the 1920s? They were several. First, as we have seen, the central myth was that France could by its own efforts maintain the European system in equilibrium. Ever since 1870, the central equation of European politics had been that of Germany and France. The decision of 1918 had reversed that of 1870 in as much as France was this time on the victorious side and regained the territories of Alsace and Lorraine. The desire for revenge that had been such a conspicuous element in France's outlook during the Third Republic from 1870 to 1914, appeared to have been satisfied. But, of course, whereas Prussia had defeated France in 1870 in a direct contest, France had only gained her revenge against Germany as part of a successful coalition that also included Britain, Russia for a time and subsequently the United States. However, the future balance of Europe after 1919 was to depend on an assumption that France could by herself serve as a check and a counterweight to Germany. This was an assumption that, given the increasing discrepancy in industrial power between the two countries and the stagnation in France's population growth, was becoming increasingly unrealistic.

The second myth of the period followed on from the logic of the first one: that was that Europe was still sufficient unto itself as far as the balance mechanism was concerned. It had been demonstrated that even the joint efforts of all the European powers combined – Britain, France, Russia and Italy – were barely sufficient to check Germany. In such a situation the traditional balance-of-power mechanism could not operate. And consequently, albeit for its own interests, the United States was co-opted into the European system and served as an adjunct of the balance mechanism.

There was a third myth and that was that the maintenance of a preponderance of power in the hands of the victor powers was equated with an effective League of Nations. As long as France was dedicated to the *status quo* that provided her security and as long as France was the predominant military power on the continent – which in view of Germany's forced disarmament she was – no power could challenge the 1919 settlement. And this was interpreted as indicating that the League of Nations was

operating successfully to avoid war. Clearly, the optimism of the period of the 1920s was unfounded. It was the function of the League to produce peaceful settlement of disputes between states. And it was apparent that the most serious disputes would arise with respect to revision of the 1919 treaties. The point is, of course, that there was no military challenge to the treaties in the 1920s because the revisionist powers – those left dissatisfied by the 1919 settlement – did not then have the military capacity to challenge the treaties. The test of the League came in the 1930s when disputes could be, and were, settled by military means. When this occurred the League failed abysmally for the simple reason that, if collective security depended on preponderance of power, those states that supported the League no longer possessed this margin of superiority.

The joint product of all these myths put together was the over-arching myth of the 1920s: the persisting belief that somehow states were living up to the ideals of the covenant and were no longer operating purely in terms of the old immoral power considerations. So powerful was this myth that a whole elaborate diplomatic framework was established to enshrine it. First, there was the machinery of the League itself. During the latter 1920s, it experienced its most successful period as the talking-shop of Europe's statesmen. It was fortunate that several of the leading figures of the times developed a regular habit of attending at Geneva and participating in the debates, the period of the so-called 'Geneva Spirit'. But if we were to be cynical we might point to the fact that this same period was to witness the League suffering from severe financial constraints, which perhaps in-dicated that although all the states saw the value in being members of the club, when it came to the crunch they were none too willing to pay their subscriptions.

Apart from the League itself, there was during the 1920s an entire stream of diplomacy that was carried on at the level of mythology. There were the endless disarmament debates of the 1920s and early 1930s. Why should we consign them to the level of mythology? Because the very fact that the powers considered the time ripe for disarmament talks suggested that the basic problems of European security had been solved: whereas the course that the talks took, in practice, revealed only too clearly

the context of extreme insecurity in which these discussions were taking place. The evidence for this is overwhelming. Each power saw the disarmament question in the light of the impact that it would have on its own defensive capacity. Each power came up with definitions of military power that would call for restraint of other parties but leave its own forces intact. In short, each of the powers could come up with the most sophisticated technical reasons for doing itself a good turn.

There were to be numerous other manifestations of diplomacy at the level of mythology during the 1920s. There was the Geneva Protocol of 1924, which was an attempt to strengthen the arbitration procedures of the League. Most conspicuous of all was the Kellogg pact of 1928, which was a solemn declaration by the states to refrain from using war as an instrument of policy. One need only compare the ease with which all the states signed this document with the slow, grinding lack of progress on disarmament to appreciate where the true concerns of the powers lay.

It is part of the conventional mythology that the 1920s were just beginning to show signs of fulfilment of these lofty ideals when circumstances unfortunately intervened to upset the happy course of events. The promise of the 1920s was lost because of the economic crisis of 1929 and the resurgence of militarism in Italy, Japan and Germany: the gradual fulfilment of the League ideals was suddenly, in 1931, checked by the Japanese takeover of Manchuria. Nothing of course, could be further from the truth. Such a view of the inter-war period can only be sustained by mistaking the mythology of the 1920s for the underlying reality. Moreover, there certainly was a level of reality that, as has been said, managed to coexist with the mythology for some years, but was in stark contrast to all the ideals and all the aspirations of the Geneva spirit and to all the claims of the creators of the League.

The change from the 1920s to the 1930s did not represent a transition from internationalism to conventional power politics. There was a change but that was not in the role of power so much as in the distribution of power. This brings us back to the original point that the inter-war period rested on an elaborate fiction. It was these various fictions that from 1919 itself ensured that the mythology of internationalism, peace and harmony would be supplemented by more realistic and practical measures. If the post-war structure

rested on a fiction of security that produced the League discussions, disarmament talks, the Geneva Protocol and the Kellogg pact, then the underlying reality was one of insecurity that in turn was to produce a solid stratum of *Realpolitik* throughout both the 1920s and 1930s. While this stratum coexisted with the mythology in the 1920s, in the 1930s this stratum came to the surface and swept away the mythology.

It is this underlying level of *Realpolitik* in the inter-war period that must now be considered. It can be done in three contexts:

(1) in the context of French security policy;
(2) in the context of Britain's attitude to France and to Germany;
(3) in the context of the Soviet Union's relations with Germany.

France's search for security was a prominent feature of the Versailles peace talks and of the entire post-war period and the reason why France became so concerned about her security was obvious enough. As we have seen, the settlement was based on an assumption that France could act as a counterweight to Germany, an assumption that was doubted by France herself. But unfortunately, to strengthen France's position against Germany, France was in fact offered not the tangible instruments of security but rather that promise of security that derived from the mythology of the period. France at Versailles sought to achieve certain very specific and very concrete objectives from the settlement. She sought to take the Rhineland away from Germany and so improve France's strategic position on her eastern border. This she was denied. She attempted to give the League of Nations some teeth by having that organisation set up an international military force, but again was unsuccessful. Finally she sought and was offered an Anglo-American guarantee of her eastern border only to see this guarantee lapse when the American Senate refused to ratify the Versailles treaty. Having failed in all these efforts, what did France receive by way of compensation? She received the same guarantee of security that was offered to all the states under this system – the guarantee of collective security as embodied in the League of Nations. However, it was a collective security that had to depend for its enforcement, not – as the theory required – on an absolute preponderance of power, but on the power of Britain and France.

Faced with this situation, France quickly appreciated the hollowness of her own victory and proceeded to adopt traditional measures. She did this in various ways. First, she called for strict adherence of Germany to the Versailles clauses as one means of preventing a German revival. If the balance between France and Germany at this time was an artificial one, then for France's sake it must be kept artificial. France was, therefore, the great champion of rigid and strict enforcement of the most punitive clauses of the settlement and especially of the reparations clauses. In fact, it was this subject that was to give France the excuse she required in 1923 to invade the Ruhr. If the ostensible purpose of this exercise was to enforce the provisions of the peace treaty, the real reason was French determination to keep Germany down by any means, including display of military force.

There were other signs that under the facade of the League, France had reverted to traditional balance-of-power diplomacy. In 1921 she signed an alliance with Poland and then associated herself with the Little Entente – that grouping of Eastern European states that consisted of Czechoslovakia, Rumania and Yugoslavia. An alliance in the east was the time-honoured French device for countering a threat from Germany. And the culminating example of traditional French tactics was to come in 1935 when France signed a pact with the Soviet Union. Here at last was the revival of the Franco-Russian entente that had been the feature of French foreign policy in the years preceding the First World War. In some ways it was only a shadow of that former alliance, as both signatories to the pact had strong ideological reservations about it. But the strategic situation that gave rise to it was precisely the same as that of 1894.

If France, immediately after the Versailles settlement, quickly reverted to traditional *Realpolitik* tactics, she was not alone in this. Britain, too, in her attitude towards France and Germany witnessed a revival of her traditional ambition to serve as the balancer for the European continent. In fact, the re-emergence of this British desire to act as a balancer sprang from the same origins as did the intellectual grounds for appeasement. The emergence of these feelings can be followed in Martin Gilbert's study, *The Roots of Appeasement*, in which he traces the origins of appeasement from the British reaction to the First World War and to the Versailles settlement. There was a powerful section of

British opinion that did not share the French inclination to impose a punitive treaty on Germany and thought that the Versailles treaty was over-severe. Appeasement was born then, as Gilbert shows, from a feeling that German demands for revision of the treaty were justified. This feeling increased with the publication by John Maynard Keynes of his *The Economic Consequences of the Peace* in which he argued against the severity of the reparations clauses of the treaty.

In the few years after 1919, Britain and France moved even further apart on the question of the Versailles settlement, France demanding strict adherence to its clauses and Britain, on the other hand, being prepared to allow controlled revision of the treaty. It would be wrong to imagine that the only motive of British policy was a moral reaction against the treaty. In fact, it seems clear that Britain was at this time not at all happy about French predominance in Europe, however artificial it might be, and was guided by her traditional objective of maintaining a balance on the continent. This could only be done by permitting a limited revival of German power. Clearly, on this crucial issue, Britain and France were diametrically opposed. But Britain was able on this occasion to have her way for the simple reason that France could not afford to antagonise her unduly. The great symbol of this British attempt to establish a more natural balance between Germany and France was the Locarno treaty of 1925. As a result of its provisions, Britain agreed to guarantee France's eastern frontier, and Germany undertook not to violate this frontier. This was one side of the bargain in which France's demands for security were met. The other side was the execution of the first stage of removal of foreign forces from the Rhineland. Again, the treaty was linked with Germany's admission to the League of Nations, which occurred in 1926. So, to this extent, it met Germany's demands for a revival of her international status. As guarantor of the treaty, it was clear that Britain had engineered this balance exercise. The balance that came out of this bargain was characterised by a limited rebirth of German power and a limited decline in French power; this trend towards equilibrium was controlled and checked by Britain as the holder of the balance. It is, of course, this view of British policy in the inter-war period that has led some to say that Britain contributed

to the outbreak of war by failing to pursue this role of balancer to its logical conclusion. According to this argument, just as Britain had reacted in the 1920s against French preponderance by aiding the revival of Germany, so in the 1930s Britain should have reacted to the changing balance between Germany and France so as to prevent the emerging German preponderance.

Underlying the facade of the League, there was a reversion to typical diplomatic devices on the part of both France and Britain. Another conspicuous example of traditional power-tactics at this period is that provided by German–Soviet relations. It was one of the aims of the League of Nations to prevent the formation of rival international alignments and so a recurrence of the alliance patterns of the pre-1914 generation. In this aim, the League conspicuously failed. No sooner did it exclude the defeated Germany and Soviet Russia from the League as international outcasts, than these two powers came together and signed a treaty at Rapallo in 1922. In fact, as the Rapallo treaty was to demonstrate, German–Soviet relations were to provide the classic examples of balance-of-power considerations. This can be seen in the Rapallo treaty itself. For both of the signatories, the treaty was seen as a way out of the diplomatic isolation in which they had been left as a result of the war and of the revolution. More particularly, Germany needed Russia in order to overcome the disarmament provisions of the Versailles treaty, as the Soviet Union during the 1920s was to become the main area in which Germany carried out military training and tests on her military equipment. From the Soviet point of view, alliance with Germany was welcomed because the Soviet nightmare was of a united capitalist offensive against the Soviet state. Given this fear, the only tactic available to her was to exploit such divisions as existed within the capitalist camp and at this particular period, the main division was between the victors on the one hand and Germany on the other.

German–Soviet relations were to pass through several stages in the course of the two decades of the inter-war period. And at each stage both powers were guided by their ambivalent attitude towards the western powers. For Germany's part, she had turned to the Soviet Union in 1922 to overcome her international isolation. What brought the partnership to an end was Hitler's

rise to power in Germany. By this time, Germany had succeeded in wedging herself in between the West and the Soviet Union and in exploiting her geographical position by playing the one off against the other. How she managed to do so was a result largely of the ambiguous ideological standing of Hitler and of the Nazi movement in Germany. There is in fact a fairly close parallel between the role played by Nazism in German domestic affairs and that on the international scene. It can be argued that in both instances, by a deliberate tactic of confusing accepted political differentiations, Nazism pretended to defend the system as a pretext for in fact overthrowing it. Domestically, it adopted an ambiguous platform on social policy such as to appeal to left and to right, to the workers and to the industrialists. To the masses, Hitler promised a social revolution and at the same time one of Hitler's strongest appeals was as Germany's defender against communism. When Hitler came to power in 1933 both the radicals in his own party and the representatives of the old order in Germany thought that their voice would now be heard. Likewise, on the international scene, Germany made use of her ambiguous posture. She appealed to the Soviet Union as a fellow-outcast – one of the dissatisfied powers of Europe – and at the same time looked towards the west with her capitalist face, claiming to be the western bastion against communism. It is quite clear that many European statesmen, including Churchill, welcomed Hitler's accession to power for precisely the reason that he would check any expansion of communism into Europe.

If all the major European states were playing a fairly traditional power-game under the guise of internationalist rhetoric, the Soviet Union likewise was playing a fairly traditional game under the rhetoric of international revolution. She came to terms with Germany to prevent capitalist encirclement of the Soviet state. But once the German danger revived under Hitler, the Soviet Union reverted to the historical tactic of the alliance with France. Also, having despised the League of Nations in its early years, as a direct consequence of the emergence of Hitler the USSR joined the League and became one of its most loyal members.

There are many questions that can be asked about the inter-war period. Interest in the period can be expressed by asking why

the League of Nations failed, why war broke out in Europe once again, or why there was a return to power politics in the 1930s. The question can be phrased in several different ways but basically it is the same question that is being asked. Although the details of the answers may differ, they all have a common origin in the picture of the international situation that has just been described.

The League failed to function in accordance with the ideal for the reason that it was directed towards the satisfaction of narrow national self-interests: by all the victors through the exclusion of Germany; by America, through turning her back on it; more fundamentally, by the antagonistic conceptions of it held by France and by Britain, and by their respective attempts to tailor the guarantee function of the League to these conceptions.

There was, then, no return to power in the inter-war years for the simple reason that there had never been a departure from it. What then distinguishes the easy optimism of the 1920s from the tragedy of the 1930s? The answer lies not in a return to power politics but in the restoration of German power to limits more realistically aligned to its potential – in other words in the overthrow of the artificial balance of the 1920s.

The confusion has arisen as a result of the failure to distinguish a return to power from an alteration to the *status quo* of 1919. The subjugation of Germany was an intrinsic part of that *status quo*, which represented stability in post-war terms. Britain welcomed change within the system and assumed that change was compatible with the maintenance of stability. The facts of power however were such as to ensure that a change in the *status quo* would lead to instability, as Germany was potentially a stronger power than France. The problem can be illustrated as follows. The Locarno treaty has been described as an attempt to satisfy both French demands for security and German demands for revival. Given the limited sense in which Locarno permitted a German revival, this object was attained in 1925. However in the long term, and with the dimensions of Hitler's revival of Germany, the problem was insoluble because French security and German revival were essentially incompatible.

So the fundamental fact of the inter-war period was the latent power of Germany. This taught the world an important diplo-

matic lesson – that if Germany could not be contained by treaty provisions, then she must be contained by more drastic means. It was a lesson which was to lead to the division of Germany after 1945.

In conclusion, the Concert that functioned during the inter-war period was a defective one, in terms of both its restrictive membership and its operative norms. Its membership was a reduced one, above all because of the American defection, but also because of the 'exclusivist' tendency within the League's original recruitment drive.[15] Similarly, the conspicuous divergence of opinion between the major powers as to the norms of conduct on which the League was to be based resulted in an insufficient consensus upon which to base a working Concert system.

It was pointed out above that the main contribution of the Concert of Europe to the subsequent theory and practice of international order was in its tentative elaboration of a set of ground rules for the diplomatic conduct of the Great Powers: its contribution to international organisation, in the sense of tangible machinery, was negligible.

With the League of Nations, the judgement could arguably be reversed: its distinctive contribution was in the creation of the infra-structure of international organisation, to the extent of associating the League with a specific geographical location, namely Geneva. When we move on to consider the impact of the League upon the Great Powers' conceptions of international order and how they might best contribute towards it, the period strikes us as sterile. While such a judgement might appear severe, it seems nonetheless appropriate for an era in international politics that told us so much about the need for international co-operation but told us so little about how it was to be achieved. Even more, if the League experiment bequeathed any conspicuous legacies, then it was surely a disenchantment with the notion of Concert diplomacy as such: in trying to push the Concert idea too far, the League produced a widespread disillusionment with the attempt to transcend basic balance-of-power strategies. Despite the subsequent creation of the United Nations, the inter-war period represented the last occasion to date in which the powers consciously sought to construct an international order based upon norms acceptable to them all.

7 *From Concert to balance: 1945–1980*

There is a danger with this period, as with the others, in describing it as if its dominant features persist unchanged throughout several decades. Even a superficial accounting of the change of mood from 'Cold War' to 'détente' or from 'bipolarity' to 'loose bipolarity' or 'multipolarity' should convince us that this has not been the case. Nevertheless, it is possible to make some generalisations about the nature of international order in the post-Second-World-War era and about the principal modalities by means of which it has been maintained.

As with the previous chapters, the focus of discussion will be upon the diplomatic procedures and norms of the Great Powers and upon the elements of 'Concert' and 'balance' that characterised these. Above all, the conspicuous feature of the post-1945 period has been, not simply a failure to construct a working Concert system, but indeed a manifest lack of interest in trying to do so. To this extent, the period under review has much in common with the latter half of the nineteenth century or may even be regarded as a reversion to the traditions of pre-1815 days. Moreover, if this atavism was partially a product of the peculiar conditions of the age, which would have operated against Concert diplomacy in any case, it was also symptomatic of a changing intellectual mood. Despite the flurry of discussion and planning about the post-war order that persisted throughout the war years, there is little evidence of confidence that a 'brave new world' could be created. The United Nations was conceived in an age of disillusionment with mankind's capacities to shape the future and in this respect the temper of the 1940s was quite different from the early days of the League. Perhaps, in fact, recent League experience was too vivid to allow of such a sense of expectation. At any rate, Martin Wight is no doubt correct when he submits that 'the failure first of the League of Nations, and then of the permanent members of the Security Council to achieve unanimity disabused men of the idea of international order as a work of political construction'.[1]

How, then, should we characterise the main features of order

since 1945? First of all, before proceeding to discuss the specific modalities of order, a few general comments on the period are called for. The first point relates to that just made – namely, a reversion from a 'constructionist' to a *laissez-faire* attitude as far as international order is concerned. To express the same point in a slightly different form, we might say that order in the post-1945 period may well have emerged but it has seldom been consciously pursued. This, in turn, has been viewed as one of the ironies of the present age, in the sense, to quote again from Wight, that 'since 1945 a decline in theoretical concern for international order has paradoxically coincided with a balance of power that has defied pessimists by its durability'.[2] The realists would, of course, contend that this must inevitably be so. Such, at any rate, is the conviction of Henry Kissinger:

The attainment of peace is not as easy as the desire for it. Not for nothing is history associated with the figure of Nemesis, which defeats man by fulfilling his wishes in a different form or by answering his prayers too completely. Those ages which in retrospect seem most peaceful were least in search of peace. Those whose quest for it seems unending appear least able to achieve tranquility.[3]

Accordingly, Kissinger would see the tragedy of the inter-war period to lie in its over-preoccupation with instituting a novel system of order whereas the post-war world has achieved more by aspiring to less.

A second general observation on the period would be that while it has not been wholly without collectivist policies, these have been articulated in the form of collective defence arrangements rather than as a collective security apparatus. Much more obviously, and more rapidly than in the post-1919 phase, did the accoutrements of collective security give way to the substance of alliance mechanisms. The guarantee of collective security provided by the United Nations was, as we shall see, not only supplemented but supplanted by specific alliance commitments, NATO and the Warsaw pact being the foremost of these.

The third aspect to be considered is central to the continuing theme of this book and this is the nature, and the provenance, of the norms associated with the Great Powers' relations with each other. It was argued previously that the Concert of Europe had two principal facets, one asserting a special position within the

international system for the Great Powers and the other mitigating the effects of this by prescribing rules for Great-Power conduct. The latter is as central to the Concert idea as is the former. This is a point which Hedley Bull, apart from a few saving qualifications, comes close to missing. He sees the Great Powers as contributing to order in two main ways: 'by managing their relations with one another, and by exploiting their preponderance in such a way as to impart a degree of central direction to the affairs of international society as a whole'.[4] Bull then goes on to list the various means by which these two contributions are made and mentions a 'great power concert' under the second category. The whole point is, of course, that a Concert, if it is to mean anything, means also 'managing their relations with one another'. Subsequently, however, Bull makes the substantial qualification that these two Great-Power roles are closely interconnected and, by doing so, makes his formulation less open to criticism. In his own words:

> The steps the great powers take to manage their relations with one another lead directly to the attempt to provide central direction or management of the affairs of international society as a whole; the steps they take to exploit their preponderance in relation to the rest of international society presuppose some effective management of their relations with one another.[5]

Have there been norms of Great-Power behaviour in the post-1945 period? Probably the closest that we can come to such a notion is in the form of conventions limiting conflict between the Super-Powers and we might label these 'rules of crisis management', or simply 'the policy of détente'. Apart from the inherent difficulties with these terms, which will be discussed shortly, there is still the question whether these practices would be sufficient to warrant description as Concert diplomacy. At the very least, there is the doubt that a Concert can consist of two powers alone, because crisis management and détente, if, and to the extent that, they have been practised, have been norms confined solely to the two Super-Powers. Thus, Bull is correct to point out that 'it will be necessary, however, to study not only crisis avoidance and control, as it has been practised by the United States and the Soviet Union in the period of their predominance, but also to

extend the inquiry to embrace the avoidance and control of crises in a system of several great powers'.[6]

Membership of a Concert apart, there is also the issue of its content. If crisis management or détente are seen as behavioural traits of (to use Coral Bell's terminology) an 'adversary partnership', one may legitimately question whether such a partnership can constitute a Concert, especially if, as seems to have been the case for much of the post-war period, the 'adversary' element has been more visible than the 'partnership' component. The late Alaister Buchan thought not:

> The development of an awareness of parallel Soviet–American interests during the ten years since the Cuban crisis, in the sense of both tacit and explicit understanding about the rules by which deterrence can be maintained while war may be avoided, has led neither to a super power condominium ... nor to a significant expansion of the area of political detente ... The bipolar relationship remains primarily an adversary one.[7]

A fourth issue relates to whether a situation in which the dominant strategic concepts derive from a relationship of nuclear deterrence can appropriately be described as a reversion to balance-of-power practices. The distinctions between 'balance of power' and 'balance of terror' have frequently been reiterated,[8] and need not be detailed here. Suffice it to say that the debate centres upon notions of power and equilibrium in the nuclear age, on the increasing subjectivity of estimations of balance, on the decreasing importance of marginal quantities of military power and upon the changing role of alliances or alignments in such a context. It is not the intention of this chapter to argue against these propositions and to maintain that nuclear weaponry has not modified traditional balance-of-power practices. What can be said, however, is that the system of nuclear deterrence is essentially a set of precepts for counterpoising nuclear force against nuclear force in a decentralised milieu and, from that perspective, is much closer to a classical balance system than to any other variant scheme for the management of power between states. The point to be emphasised, then, is that the description of the post-war years as a 'balance' age should not be disallowed on the 'technicality' of the existence of nuclear weaponry.

Fifthly, we must consider the implications for the overall

argument of the trend, widely perceived by analysts, towards an increasingly 'multipolar' world structure, a trend beginning in the 1960s but accelerating in the 1970s. To the extent that such a development has taken place, it marks a departure from Wight's outline history in which 'though the field of the balance of power expanded the number of decisive weights has decreased'.[9] If the objection was that balance policies could not be pursued in a bipolar world, then the force of this argument has presumably declined *pari passu* with the 'tightness' of the Soviet–American polarity.

How should we best describe the polarity of the system in the 1970s? The case can be argued that we must distinguish between mere international pluralism and the number of poles of influence that give the system its main characteristics. Accordingly, the international system has become more pluralistic throughout the past two decades. However, if we had to define the essential elements in the present situation it would be in terms of a system which early in the 1970s became a fairly formalised tripolar system. The multipolar view of Nixon and Kissinger in which both Europe and Japan participate as equals may emerge in the future but it is not a reality at the moment. What has become much more of a reality in the last few years is China's international status, which places her along with the US and the USSR in the ranks of the first-line powers and not along with Japan and the European states.

The best way to justify this point of view is by showing how this situation has come about. And, as can be seen from the nature of the argument, there are two parts to it. First, we have to show how there has been a fairly continual trend throughout two decades towards international political pluralism. And secondly, we have to show how, over and above this trend, something quite specific has happened that allows us to define the present situation as a tripolar one.

At a very general level, it is an easy enough task to identify the various developments that tended to increase the element of pluralism in international life. These points are familiar and scarcely contentious. There are three facets of the trend worth mentioning:

(1) The first was the tendency towards disintegration within the two

Cold-War-camps. On the Soviet side, the first example of this was the defection of Yugoslavia but of course by far the most important example was the rift between Moscow and Peking. In the course of the 1960s Rumania joined the ranks of those eastern states that were gaining a certain amount of autonomy over their own affairs. On the western side, the most conspicuous evidence of friction within the NATO fold were the demonstrative gestures of France but this was no more than the most prominent symptom of a fairly widespread complaint. The 1960s – in the course of which many of the European countries became uneasy about the extent of American foreign investment in the European economies, also witnessed the gradual erosion of faith in America's determination to meet her nuclear guarantees. On the American side, there was growing disillusionment with the sincerity of European efforts to provide a greater contribution to their own defence. These various sources of contention came to a head during the 1960s with France actually withdrawing from NATO's organs in 1966 and in the form of a series of debates about NATO strategy in Europe.

(2) A second reason for the emergence of a more pluralistic international system may well be found in a factor that facilitated the disintegration of the monolithic appearance of the two camps. This was the very fact of the balance that existed between the two camps as the Cold War evolved into the 1950s. There is obviously a sense in which the nuclear stalemate between the two Super-Powers created greater room for manoeuvre on the part of the lesser members of the opposing alliance systems. China is the example on the one side and France the example on the other. Just as the balance between the two camps created a margin of discretion for the non-aligned states, so that same balance increased the autonomy of some of the states within the rival alliances. Another example of this is in relation to the effect of the Sino-Soviet dispute on eastern Europe. Here it is possible to see that the existence of conflict between Moscow and Peking has strengthened the bargaining hand of certain of the eastern European states, particularly Yugoslavia and Rumania.

(3) The third factor to be mentioned is the economic recovery of Europe and of Japan. At least in part, the Cold War between the USSR and the United States sprang up as a response to the economic and political collapse of Germany and Japan. If this was

the situation that gave birth to the bipolar order, then clearly by the 1960s this situation was changing rapidly as Europe and Japan reasserted their status in world economic terms.

If these were some of the developments that heightened the element of pluralism in international politics, what specific trends can be singled out as forming the basis of the argument that the present international system is best viewed as a tripolar one? Obviously, this is not a proposition that can be put forward dogmatically. Even on definitional grounds it could be objected that there is little distinction between pluralism and multi-polarity. The argument, however, would be as follows: that although there are now a multiplicity of centres in the world that make an active contribution on the international scene and have a considerable degree of autonomy in their foreign affairs, there is still a sense in which the three powers – the US, the USSR and China – are qualitatively more important in international life than any of the others.

This is true in two senses. In purely objective terms, while only the US and the USSR are important actors in every region of the globe, China is nonetheless becoming an actor of global proportions. But even more important than this objective sense is the fact that China is perceived by the Super–Powers as sharing a special triangular relationship with them – something that could not be said of Soviet or American perceptions of Japan or Europe. In other words, there has emerged fairly recently in the early 1970s, a highly formalised tripolar relationship between Washington, Moscow and Peking in which each state recognises that the most important elements of international security are bound up with her relations with the other two. Moreover, whereas there is a sense in which the US, USSR and China have always had a three-sided relationship, it is now a genuinely triangular one instead of three bilateral relationships which only marginally affect each other.

It was one of the most conspicuous features of American foreign policy in the 1960s that the existence of the Sino-Soviet dispute made little difference to the United States' relationship with either China or the Soviet Union. And neither did China nor the USSR substantially modify their postures towards the United States solely on account of the friction that was develop-

ing between them. To a large extent all three powers operated on considerations that took little account of what was happening on the other two sides of the triangle. The 1970s have, however, brought about a change in this respect in that little is now done on any one side of the triangle without a calculation as to what is happening on the other two and without a calculation as to what effect any move will have on the other two. The three powers are now functioning within a highly formalised and systematised triangular relationship that appears to be the central fact of international life at the moment. For this reason the present international system can be defined as being tripolar.

What evidence is there for the view that these three states are now conducting their diplomacy in such a way that there is a formalised triangular relationship between them? There are at least three pieces of evidence that this is the case. In the first place, on the American side, the major consideration that led to a rapprochement between the United States and China was the relationship between the United States and the Soviet Union. In the second place, as far as China was concerned, it was Russia who prompted her to come to an accommodation with America. And in the third place, the major limitation upon the extent of this rapprochement between Washington and Peking is the bilateral relationship between Washington and Moscow.

How are we to justify these three assertions? As the 1960s came to an end and the 1970s began, the United States found increasingly that in her dialogue with the Soviet Union, her bargaining position was deteriorating. One example of this was the SALT talks. The reasons why the American position was deteriorating are attributable to several factors, probably the most important of which was the continuing drain of the Vietnam war. At the very time when the US seemed less willing to meet her global commitments, the Soviet Union was extending hers – particularly in the Middle East and in the Indian subcontinent.

The culmination of these various trends was that for the first time the United States decided to avail herself of the opportunity presented to her by the Sino-Soviet dispute and to improve her bargaining position *vis-à-vis* Moscow by initiating a dialogue with Peking. This was the most basic consideration underlying the Nixon visit to Peking in 1972 and the admission of China to the United Nations.

Russian sources provide several clear statements as to how the Sino-American rapprochement was viewed in Moscow. By China's admission to the United Nations and as a result of the Nixon visit, Peking's status in international terms was greatly increased. Indeed, such an increase in status was the price that Washington had to pay for Peking's agreement to enter into a dialogue that would demonstrate to Moscow that, if the USSR became too ambitious, she would have to face joint opposition to her on the part of America and China. A few quotes from Russian sources make this point very well. According to one Soviet analyst what the United States was seeking to do was to 'meet half way the Maoists' great power claims and style and to persuade the world public that Washington really regards Peking as a full-fledged global partner'.[10] The reason why she was doing so was that 'the present stage is characterised by a further weakening of the USA's position and prestige in international affairs. In the confrontation with the Soviet Union ... US imperialism now seeks new partners and Washington is trying to find such a partner in China.'[11] By the nature of her overtures to Peking the United States sought to promote the emergence of a tripolar system within which the Soviet Union could be more effectively checked than by the continuance of the purely bipolar arrangement. To quote again from a Soviet commentator, 'the endeavour to stimulate the globalisation of the Chinese factor is closely connected with the adoption of a triangular foreign policy stance ... China is wedging itself into the traditional structure of the present day world and in doing so is transforming this structure by introducing a new additional coefficient of complexity into foreign policy calculations.'[12] This is to say that it would no longer be sufficient to operate on the basis of purely bilateral considerations.

The second point was that China's main motivation in coming to terms with Washington was the state of her own relations with the USSR. There is no suggestion that this was the sole calculation on Peking's part. However, it does seem to be a reasonable assumption that the border fighting between China and Russia in the spring of 1969, followed by the build-up of the Soviet forces along the Chinese border, was an important consideration in the formulation of the new policy towards the United States. There were other elements in the equation that facilitated a rapproche-

ment with the US, such as the apparent American determination to withdraw her military forces from Asia, but the main motive was the tension on the Sino-Soviet border.

The third point was that the main limitation upon the Sino-American rapprochement was the bilateral dialogue between the Soviet Union and America. The United States had to be very careful that in developing a relationship with Peking she did not push it too far, with the negative result that the dialogue with Moscow would have been destroyed. At the end of the 1960s, Soviet–American relations were in an ambivalent condition, elements of both rivalry and co-operation being present. The rivalry was in relation to overall international position and although this rivalry was not acute, it was capable of becoming so, as was to be demonstrated in South Asia in 1971 and in the Middle East in 1973. At the same time, the two powers had embarked on a bilateral dialogue on a whole range of important issues. There were the SALT talks themselves. There were the negotiations for a European security conference and for balanced force-reductions in Europe. There were negotiations for the expansion of trade between the two countries. All these aspects of Soviet–American relations could have been placed in jeopardy by the Sino–American rapprochement if it had been carried too far.

To summarise, there is a much more pluralistic distribution of influence within the system. But just as the bipolar set-up was characterised by one defining quality – what one analyst has termed the dominance of the 'relationship of major tension', i.e. the Soviet–American confrontation – now it makes little sense to consider Soviet–American relations in isolation from China because China has become so much a part of that relationship. In other words, if there is still a relationship of major tension in international politics, then it is effectively a tripolar one. As such there is no *prima facie* reason why it should not be a system in which balance considerations are prominent.

The sixth general point by way of comment on the post-1945 international order pertains to the very concept of security at the present time. According to some accounts, governments are no longer concerned simply to further the ends of military security but tend to define their security increasingly in economic or 'welfare' terms. It follows from such an interpretation that inter-

national politics can no longer be thought to be coextensive with the field of deterrence or strategy and that any concentration on the purely 'military balancing' component of international order is misleading as a general depiction of the age.

The argument is compelling and has had many adherents. It is as a result of this line of reasoning that Herz reaches his conclusion that 'the event which led to the destruction of the balance system was the growing, and now worldwide, interconnection of economic and other relationships in the industrial age and the ensuing interdependence of states'.[13] Keohane and Nye have dubbed this a situation of 'complex interdependence' and more strongly than most argue that 'balance of power theories and national security imagery are also poorly adapted to analysing problems of economic or ecological interdependence. Security, in traditional terms, is not likely to be the principal issue facing governments.'[14]

We may accept the general drift of these arguments but it is unclear what their implications are for the present discussion. Even if it is conceded that the distinction between 'high' and 'low' politics is inappropriate under current conditions and that the issues that face present-day governments are distinctively novel, as is the setting of interdependence in which these issues have to be confronted, this need not, however, imply that statecraft itself has been revolutionised. In fact, a superficial survey of international economic and 'resources' diplomacy in the 1970s suggests that the continuities of 'power politics' are as striking as are their modifications.

It has been argued by many scholars that international relations are not susceptible of a progressivist interpretation – that the element of morality in international political practice has not increased appreciably over the centuries. On the evidence of recent international responses to questions of ecology and distribution of scarce resources, there is reason for thinking that these scholars are not wrong.

In the last few years, there has, according to the interdependence theorists just mentioned, been a pronounced change of emphasis in the nature of the problems that have vexed the world's statesmen. While traditional issues of a politico-strategic nature have not faded from the scene, they have in many

instances been temporarily obscured by more pressing demands in the international economic sphere.

What placed economic issues at the head of summit agendas was the confluence of at least three discrete developments. The first was the intrusion into the world's consciousness that all might not be well with mankind's relationship to his environment – as one writer has phrased it, 'by the early 1970's, the macro-ecologists were gathering full voice and, in March of 1972, when the Club of Rome issued the Meadows' Limits of Growth, they reached high C'.[15] The second was the specific element in the 'Doomsday Syndrome', which emphasised the finiteness of certain key resources. And the third development was the tangible experience of the post-October-1973 oil crisis, which was important because it appeared, however erroneously, to validate the general 'attrition of resources' argument.

The elevation of these economic issues to the forefront of international politics was in itself a significant occurrence. However, what was even more interesting was the common property that was shared by each of these problems: the striking feature of these challenges was that they required a concerted international effort to meet them.

This was scarcely an unprecedented situation as far as the world's diplomats were concerned, but, given the urgency of the questions involved, it did serve once again to throw into sharp relief the limitations of the present political organisation of the globe when confronted with tasks that transcend national boundaries.

While this has been a perennial facet of international life, it seemed to weigh more oppressively than ever on the collective mind of the early 1970s. If the main emphasis of the environmentalists and of the economic pundits was on the interrelatedness of all things, on eco-systems and economic interdependence, then how were states to respond to this situation?

In previous historical eras, the traditional *riposte* of the state to challenges to her security has been a twofold one. On the one hand, states have generally fallen back on their own capabilities and pursued, individually, what was taken to be their own national interests. As a counterpoint to this, on the other hand, there has been a trend towards greater international co-opera-

tion, be it in the form of alliances, collective security or schemes for world government.

The past half-century, since the inauguration of the League of Nations, has witnessed the uneasy co-existence of these two trends: the latter, the international-community approach, constituting the theory, and the former, the autonomous pursuit of national interest, constituting the bulk of the international practice.

What strikes the observer is that this pattern, with respect to traditional politico-strategic concerns, has recently been duplicated with respect to the ecological concerns of 'planet earth', and in response to the resources issue in particular. Once again, if international co-operation has provided the ideal and the rhetoric, the *sauve qui peut* mentality that places national salvation first, has undoubtedly become the behavioural norm.

Where is the rhetoric of international co-operation in the face of this economic challenge? Astonishingly, the purveyors of this rhetoric have not taken the trouble to find their own terminology, but have simply adopted the utopian catch-phrases of the 1920s. Just as President Wilson advocated collective security as a substitute for 'power politics', so the modern idealists are spreading the gospel of 'collective economic security'.[16]

However, no sooner had the spectre of resource depletion been raised, than the phrase 'resources diplomacy' was coined. It is said that the Chinese character for the word 'crisis' denotes both 'danger' and 'opportunity'. The same might well be said of the word 'scarcity'. One state's vulnerability is another state's leverage. This is not to deny that resource-producers and resource-consumers have a shared economic interest. It does, however, suggest that should this interest be clouded by political considerations, the outcome is as likely to be competition as co-operation.

During the 1970s, the principal example we have of this relationship in operation is OPEC and the oil crisis. Whatever the unique facets of this relationship, the experience indicates that whereas resource scarcity could lead to international co-operation, there is a more than even chance that it will be grist to the international conflictual mill.

The second piece of evidence, which indicates that the question of world resources is as likely to produce the autonomous pursuit

of self-interest as the construction of a system of collective economic security, can be found in the response of the industrialised
states to the Arab oil-embargo in 1973. In the heat of the crisis,
each major power instantly looked to its own interests. Japan
quickly saw the rectitude of the Arab case, and Britain and
France, more beholden to the Arabs for oil than the United
States, and politically less attached to Israel, found it impossible
to see eye-to-eye with Washington.

We are thus faced with the hard fact that even in relatively
homogeneous and integrated communities such as the European
and North Atlantic, definitions of economic security will tend to
differ, and that this will be reflected in political stances that take
little heed of supra-national norms.

The third aspect of contemporary world politics that demonstrates the impact of the resources issue, and the effect that the
'Great Oil Sheikdown' has had in international life, likewise
provides no comfort for the optimists. Far from enhancing any
conception of 'only one earth', and of propagating moves towards
a more egalitarian international ethic, the energy crunch and its
economic ramifications have had a regressive effect on international moral standards. Nowhere is this more apparent than in
the plight of the developing non-oil-producing countries in the
aftermath of October 1973 and in the developed world's reactions
to that plight. So obsessed has the developed world become with
putting its own economic house in order that, in the words of one
critic, 'dominant western opinion is not just disillusioned over
development, it has almost stopped considering it'.[17]

Whereas the industrialised West used to feel responsible and
mildly guilty about the underdeveloped countries, they now no
longer even feel responsible. The tendency is towards creeping
autarky and autonomy rather than towards spreading internationalism. In part, this neo-mercantilist approach has been
produced by the specific economic consequences of the oil crisis.
But it also has a more general source in the logical implications
that flowed from the ecological and resource-depletion outcries of
the early 1970s. Underlying the traditional mythology associated
with development aid was the notion of an infinitely expandable
economic universe in which all states, both developed and developing, could march forward together into the sunset of the

consumer millennium. Into this splendid vision, the ecologists introduced a rather jarring note: if resources were finite, then the context in which states pursued their economic destinies was not one of 'mutual gain' but one of 'zero-sum' in which one's gain was likely to be the other's loss.

And so here was yet another instance where the environmental situation, far from providing a unifying impulse, had, if anything, divided international society more deeply and drawn the lines between the various sectors more starkly.

The fourth illustration requires little elaboration. If the hope of the optimists was that a shared perception of ecological doom might instil a new international ethos into the diplomatic arena, then the indications are that the trend is in the reverse direction. The hoary old notion of the supreme value adhering to the national interest has taken on a new lease of life, to the point where the use of force in defence of the national economic interest was portrayed as legitimate. If we were to believe Messrs Ford and Kissinger that the United States would not allow the western world to be 'strangled' by an oil embargo, we are faced with a redefinition of the rules of the diplomatic game in the classic *Realpolitik* style.

For the past four centuries, the levers of economic power have remained in the hands of the western world. Now, it appears, some of the leading industrialised states find it intolerable that economic weapons should be turned against themselves. The cynic must be forgiven for detecting an ironic note in the moral indignation with which many Americans have greeted the activities of OPEC. This surely reflects the persistence of international moral anarchy when states attempt to redefine the boundaries of acceptable diplomatic behaviour in accordance with their own political and economic interests.

The recent international response to the resources question augurs ill for 'spaceship earth'. If the ecological and economic problems posed in the past few years have demanded new levels of concerted international action, then the practice has been true to traditional 'power political' form.

While the context of international politics has taken on a whole new dimension, there can be little doubt that the classical modes of state behaviour still predominate. Despite the rhetoric of the

new economic diplomacy, one is left with a strong impression of *plus ça change, plus c'est la même chose.*

It is now time to move on and consider the specific modalities of order-maintenance in the post-1945 world and, on the basis of that evidence, to try to characterise the main international political procedures of the age. Although almost every aspect of international life has some impact on the nature of the present order, this discussion will be confined to the following topics: international organisations and the United Nations; nuclear deterrence; spheres of influence; and crisis management and 'détente'.

INTERNATIONAL ORGANISATIONS AND THE UNITED NATIONS

It is difficult to assess the role and contribution of international organisations in recent international politics and even more so to speculate about their potential role. Judgements about these organisations consequently tend to vary from the 'power politics in disguise' verdict at one end of the spectrum to the 'incipient world community' at the other, and from seeing international organisations as passive reflections of the state of political play to seeing them as active participants and potential vehicles of change. Keohane and Nye, for instance, believe that international organisations function differently and have a more important role in a world of 'complex interdependence'. As they themselves have argued the case,

in a world of multiple issues imperfectly linked, in which coalitions are formed transnationally and transgovernmentally, the potential role of international institutions in political bargaining is greatly increased. In particular, they help set the international agenda, and act as catalysts for coalition formation and as arenas for political initiatives and linkage by weak states.[18]

It would, of course, be premature to make any definitive pronouncement upon international organisations and Inis Claude, in discussing the vast quantitative proliferation of these organisations, best reflects the ambivalent, and tentative, nature of our assessment of them:

At the very least, this growth suggests that statesmen are now more willing to emphasize collective rather than merely unilateral approaches to a wide range of issues. At most, it may presage the development of a more effective system for the management of international relations than the world has yet known. In promoting the proliferation of international agencies and the greater scope and variety of their activities, states neither guarantee that result nor provide unequivocal evidence of their dedication to its achievement, but they at least open up the possibility of its achievement.[19]

If we focus exclusively upon the United Nations, we have the same problem with general assessments but can also make some specific, and less equivocal, observations.

There is a fairly wide consensus amongst analysts of the UN that there have been, broadly speaking, three distinctive phases in the evolution of the UN's operations. The first of these did not last beyond the original conception of the UN, as the philosophy of the Charter was quickly overtaken by developments in international politics and by the outbreak of the Cold War in particular. The second phase of UN activities is associated with the use of that organisation as an instrument of western policy: the period was marked by a large western majority and the use to which this was put was best, if unusually, displayed by the Korean war. The third phase started in the mid-1950s and has, in a sense, lasted ever since: this witnessed the great numerical expansion in UN membership, especially from the Afro-Asian countries, the disappearance of the west's automatic majority, the greater attention devoted to issues of development and the emergence of a new peacekeeping role for the organisation in the shape of small 'policing' ventures rather than the large interventions symbolised by the Korean episode.

The original Charter was, to a large extent, devised on the assumption of a continuance of the Great-Power co-operation of the war period. The major role in assuring international order was assigned to the Security Council, which was to be composed of eleven members, six of which would be temporary and five of which would be permanent and of these, clearly the permanent members were pre-eminent – the United States, the Soviet Union, Britain, France and China. If these powers were unanimous on some issue, they could authorise actions binding on the remainder of the UN's membership.

That the Charter placed authority for the future supervision of the international system explicitly in the hands of the Great Powers can scarcely be denied and was amply revealed in the provision that granted the permanent members of the Security Council a veto. This veto was to ensure that the collective security provisions of the Charter could not be applied by one Great Power against another or that the UN could not be used to impose a settlement on a Great Power that dissented from a UN verdict. Inis Claude has developed this point when he argued that

the insertion of the veto provision in the decision-making circuit of the Security Council reflected the clear conviction that in cases of sharp conflict among the great powers the Council ought, for safety's sake, to be incapacitated – to be rendered incapable of being used to precipitate a showdown or to mobilise collective action against the recalcitrant power. The philosophy of the veto is that it is better to have the Security Council stalemated than to have that body used by a majority to take action so strongly opposed by a dissident great power that a world war is likely to ensue.[20]

As originally conceived, the UN was, we can see, based on several principles: first, that overall supervision of security matters should be the firm responsibility of the major powers; secondly, that the UN should not be used against an unwilling Great Power; and thirdly that the UN should have some 'teeth', a development considered necessary in view of the experience of the League of Nations. As part of this effort, the Charter envisaged the creation of a Military Staff Committee, composed of military personnel from the member states of the Security Council.

As noted, the UN embodied in the Charter did not materialise, as it was quickly overtaken by the Cold War. This resulted in a peacekeeping role for the UN quite different from the one originally intended, as a dynamic UN role was very much dependent upon a level of agreement between the Super-Powers that greatly surpassed that which was possible in the atmosphere of the Cold War. This also had the effect of preventing the fruition of the military clauses of the Charter. Under the circumstances, it is not surprising that the peacekeeping role of the UN should have been tailored and have moved away from a full-scale system of collective security to one in which the UN does little

more than provide small-scale emergency 'policing' and 'supervisory' units.

At the level of general assessments of UN performance, we have the same ambivalent attitude with which international organisations as a whole have been regarded. In Goodwin's terminology, it depends very much upon whether one holds to an 'organic' or 'instrumental' view of the organisation, the first seeing it as an 'incipient world community capable of spontaneous growth'[21] and the latter seeing it 'as the instrument of its leading members, to be used as they see fit'.[22]

LeRoy Bennett also arrives at an uncertain judgement:

At the present stage of history, the United Nations system of agencies ... provide a bridge between the old and the new world order. On the one hand, they act as a conservative force against radical change by conforming to the status quo and by further institutionalising the present international framework. On the other hand, they reflect the necessity for olderly, cooperative action in attacking the common problems of humanity.[23]

If we move on to specific aspects of the United Nations, it is, however, possible to be more positive. We can, for instance, clearly perceive how the UN fits into the concept of Concert diplomacy developed in this study: it fits not at all well. In fact, if we concentrate on the veto provisions of the Security Council, a case could be mounted for the view that the United Nations is predicated upon an explicit rejection of any notion of Concert diplomacy.

How is this so? We have noted that it is a part of the Concert idea that the Great Powers, in their relations with each other, should adhere to certain precepts of behaviour – in the European Concert, the most important of these being the requirement of formal and common consent to change. This is to say that in Concert diplomacy, the powers adhere to some kind of group norm. But the veto provision can be understood only as a statement that, as far as the major powers are concerned, there shall be no such group norm. While the organisational principle for the security of the remainder of international society shall be a collective one, for the Great Powers it is to be strongly individualistic. Moreover, such norms of behaviour as are to apply to international society, such as peaceful settlement of disputes, are not to be enforced upon the Great Powers them-

selves. It is in this sense, presumably, that Martin Wight made his comment that 'the Great Power veto written into the new international constitution in 1944–5 divorced the notion of the balance of power from the notion of international order'.[24] The balance of power was to be liberated from the artificial constraints of such formal principles as are characteristic of Concert diplomacy. There is, therefore, a touch of primitivism, if also of realism, in the *carte blanche* that the major powers were accorded by the terms of the UN Charter.

It followed logically that the balance of power would bypass the UN forum and manifest itself elsewhere. There is, therefore, an important sense in which the Charter's denial of Concert diplomacy has made a major impression on the subsequent peacekeeping history of the organisation and this is in the divorce between 'order' and 'power' referred to by Wight and the consequent loss of real power by the UN. As one commentator has pointed out 'in contrast to the intention to draw collective security forces mainly from the great powers, the practice in peacekeeping has been to insulate each situation from major-power involvement, influence or confrontation'.[25] This does not mean that 'power' is no longer exercised or of importance, only that it is exercised outside the UN rather than within it.

NUCLEAR DETERRENCE

As the nuclear 'balance of terror' is a pervasive component of the post-1945 international order, some comments must be made upon it. To the extent that the post-war order is a hierarchical one in which the Great Powers enjoy privileges commensurate with their status, this has been reinforced by the unequal distribution of nuclear force throughout international society.

Nuclear weaponry has intruded itself into international political processes in various ways, modifying our conceptions of war and our ideas about the political uses of violence. One of the most famous treatises on the nature of war was that produced by the Prussian soldier and philosopher von Clausewitz in the aftermath of the Napoleonic wars. His book *On War* is probably best remembered because it contains the well-known dictum that war is the continuation of politics by other means. This was in fact the

basic thesis of the work. What Clausewitz did was to describe the essence of war and he did so in terms that emphasised the political ends that war was intended to achieve. In writing his book, Clausewitz discussed his subject as if war was, in fact, subject to political constraints but what he should perhaps have been saying is that war ought to be subject to such constraints. Thus he writes in one place that 'the political object, as the original motive of the war, will be the standard for determining both the aim of the military force and also the amount of effort to be made'. This is a statement that wars do not follow their own military logic but are subject to political supervision and that it is political decisions that will determine the course and the extent of the war.

Clausewitz was able to write about war as if this was its fundamental nature because he generalised from the actual experience of the eighteenth century. What Clausewitz believed to be inherent in the very nature of war was little more than a historical accident produced by a set of fortuitous circumstances. During the eighteenth century wars were fought for limited purposes and one of the main reasons why this was so was the limited resources and the limited technology at the disposal of rival monarchs. In other words, war was a strictly political exercise not because of its inherent nature but because the constraints of the monarch's purse ensured that force would be employed only within the limits of the political ambitions and the financial resources of king or emperor.

In fact, at the very moment that Clausewitz wrote his treatise, the historical conditions that underlay this view had already begun to change dramatically. And the main source of this transformation was the French Revolution and the consequent emergence of nationalism as one of the main political forces in Europe. By placing war in the service of the nation state, nationalism was to provide a political end of over-riding legitimacy. The point is this – while political control of war was a relatively simple matter in days of limited political objectives, it was to be seriously impaired by the development of the political ideas of nationalism that justified almost any action that was in the interest of the nation state. The contradiction between these two tendencies was not at first apparent and was successfully

concealed by the practitioners of *Realpolitik* – the Bismarcks and Cavours – who managed to combine the conception of clinical warfare with the pursuit of a national – albeit still limited – interest. The contradiction could not, however, be concealed for ever. With the turn of the century, it was difficult to pretend that an expansive political end defined in nationalistic terms could be attained in harmony with rigorous political control over the military means. For the following reason – that if you decide that the survival of the nation state is the ultimate political end, then there is no logical reason for limiting any military means that will achieve this objective. In other words, once the decision to defend the state is taken, by the logic of the situation control of operations must then be handed over to the military, who will determine the course of the war in accordance with purely military considerations – the only important issue being that of victory. The central concern of the strategist was to discover how the forces at his disposal might best be employed in order to accomplish the end of destroying the enemy's army.

As a general statement, it can be argued that the net impact of nuclear weapons was to produce a striking decrease in the utility of military power in terms of its actual use. They destroyed the rational connection between the use of military means and the achievement of political ends. It might be said that technological advance was already making military operations disproportionate to the goals for which they were intended and that nuclear weapons only pushed this development to its logical conclusion. In any case, whether as a result of evolution or of the nuclear revolution, the relationship between war and politics was seen from a new perspective.

This change has occurred in two directions: there has been a militarisation of political thinking and, simultaneously, a politicisation of military thinking.

First, we will analyse the militarisation of political thinking. The most obvious outcome of the development of nuclear weapons, and of the view that these weapons were too dangerous to be employed, has been a switch in emphasis from the use of military power in war to the use of military power short of war. In other words, there has been a change of emphasis from the use of war to the threat of war. Deterrence is a continual process and

as its basic instrument is a military one, it is possible to argue that this has led to the militarisation of international political processes because the threat of nuclear war underlies any conflict between the Super-Powers.

Another way of saying the same thing is to argue that nuclear weapons have blurred the distinction between peace and war in that they have given force, by which is meant the threat of force, an increased place in the area before the outbreak of war. Because a nuclear war does not depend on a contest between two opposing forces in wartime itself, it has led to an extended period in which threats to use force are pitted against each other in time of peace. But if this blurring of the distinction between war and peace has led to the militarisation of political thinking, it has also had the opposite consequence of leading to the establishment of greater political restraints over war itself.

How has this come about? At this point it is necessary to introduce an important distinction – that between diplomacy and force. Diplomacy is a form of bargaining through negotiation. Force is an attempt to impose your own will. It is thus the very reverse of bargaining. Traditionally wars have been contests of force – the negotiations have broken down and both sides have attempted to impose their own will on the other by means of pure force. But a nuclear confrontation is not like a conventional war. It is a process of bargaining. It is, as Schelling has pointed out, not an attempt to overcome the opponent's strength by brute force but rather to structure his motives by the threat of the infliction of pain.[26] And what a state seeks from its military forces is not the power to overcome physically but the bargaining power that comes from its capacity to inflict this pain.

It is because of the inherent power of destruction of nuclear weapons that there has been a need to integrate more closely the threat of war with political objectives. If in a conventional war it is at the point of surrender that political considerations usually take over from purely military ones, and if, as we have seen, nuclear confrontation resembles this point of greatest potential violence, then obviously it is necessary that the political factor should enter the proceedings long before war has actually broken out. Unlike in a conventional war, it is no longer possible to await the outcome of a contest of military forces before initiating

a process of bargaining. Rather bargaining must run through the entire pre-war period when nuclear weapons are involved.

It is because the use of force has come to be directed against the minds of men rather than in a physical sense that the political element in force is becoming increasingly conspicuous. The sole purpose of military force is not physical coercion but an attempt to affect the intentions of the opponent through putting psychological pressures upon him. Thus even in the case of the bombs that were dropped on Japan in 1945, it can be argued that the target they were aimed at was not in fact Hiroshima or Nagasaki but the politicians in Tokyo. As a general rule then, in the writings of most contemporary strategists, it can be seen that there has been a shift in emphasis from the military use of force to its psychological use. Or as one analysis has expressed it 'the principal deficiency of the thesis of military obsolescence lies less in its depreciation of the utility of war than in its failure to appreciate the subtle and varied role of military power short of war'.[27]

It is at this stage that it becomes apparent that nuclear deterrence is based on a striking paradox. What we have seen so far is that because of the increasing disproportion between the destructive powers of nuclear weapons and any conceivable political end, the actual use of nuclear weapons in a war situation is hard to visualise. But at the same time the threat to use these weapons has come to play a greater role in international affairs. It is this distinction that some strategists refer to when they say that the *utility* of nuclear weapons should not be confused with their *usability*. While this is a distinction, it also is something of a paradox because there is something inherently improbable in such a relationship. The paradox is this: as deterrence rests on the posing of mutually credible threats, how can a credible threat be posed on the basis of weapons the use of which is incredible? Or to put it another way, the more successful deterrence is in practice, the more suspect it becomes in theory. This fundamental paradox in nuclear deterrence has been seized on by numerous writers as the following quotations will show. One study has argued that 'if the utility of war is greatly diminished or nullified, it is difficult to imagine threats of war indefinitely performing all the functions of war itself... In the long run a threat of senseless violence never carried out may loose its credibility.'[28] And again 'if the use of force has lost its utility,

and has in fact become obsolescent the threat of force may be expected to share a similar fate'.[29]

This, in turn, leads to a further paradox: that to ensure the prevention of war, the threat of it must be increased. Even worse, perhaps, is the apparent contradiction that in order that nuclear weapons will never have to be used, we must have more of them and they must be technically better.

With these few general remarks on the impact of nuclear weaponry, it remains only to summarise their significance in the context of Great-Power tutelage of the international system. Three points are worthy of mention. First, as already mentioned, possession of nuclear weaponry has emphasised the hierarchical dimension of international society, creating a new category of 'have' and 'have not' states. To that extent, by marking off a well-defined nuclear peer-group from the rest of society, it might be considered that nuclear weaponry has created a precondition of a successful Concert system since such a system depends upon the existence of an elite grouping of powers with a shared interest in managing the system and with the capacity to do so. In practice, however, beyond a staunch attempt to check the further proliferation of nuclear weapons, the nuclear powers have been too riven by disagreements in other areas to be able to give the system 'concerted' direction.

Secondly, nuclear weapons might have assisted the emergence of a Concert system by inculcating within the Great Powers an ideological consensus, in the shape of a shared body of ideas about nuclear diplomacy and a shared set of concepts about nuclear deterrence. In fact, such an ideological convergence is by no means assured and is not, in any case, irreversible: it is a continuous process that must be constantly worked at. It is from this perspective that some analysts see the major significance of arms-control dialogues, such as SALT – not that they will eventuate in any substantial reduction in weaponry but that they might assist the states involved to think about nuclear issues in a mutually intelligible fashion.

Thirdly, as argued above, in its essentials, a world of independent nuclear powers is a world in which balance considerations are characteristic. Despite the avowed devaluation of military power, the nuclear age is a *laissez-faire* one in which

various forms of force are pitted against each other. Indeed, the problems of devising any kind of centralised management or collectivised security are substantially aggravated because of the jealous reluctance to lose any degree of control over their weapons and technology on the part of the nuclear states.

SPHERES OF INFLUENCE

In this section, we will consider the role of spheres of influence in the maintenance of post-1945 international order. However, before doing so, I propose to examine the concept of imperialism in the belief that the two ideas are closely related: indeed, spheres of influence may be seen as a specific manifestation of the more general phenomenon of imperialism. Additionally, both concepts are open to the same difficulties of definition and interpretation.

The main problem with the idea of imperialism is as follows. If we look at the second half of the nineteenth century and especially the period 1880–1900, thought by many to represent the zenith of imperialistic activity, we find that its most striking feature was the annexation and partition of overseas territories by the European powers. Britain acquired Burma, France seized Indo-China and various islands in the Pacific. Germany too acquired territories in the Pacific. The United States annexed, amongst other places, Hawaii and the Philippines. Shortly after the turn of the century, Japan was to annexe Korea. Russia had during the 1850s and 1860s engulfed much of Central Asia and had extended her effective reach to the Pacific by the end of the century. The most dramatic partition was to occur in Africa. In 1875 only 10% was controlled by the European powers whereas by 1900 90% of Africa had been divided up amongst them. All in all, during the last quarter of the century about one-fifth of the globe fell into the possession of the European powers.

By contrast, if we look at the post-1945 period, we find that one of the salient features of the age is the break-up of the former colonial empires. The British withdrew from India and from South-East Asia. The Dutch were expelled from Indonesia, the French from Vietnam. The United States granted independence to the Philippines and in the course of the 1950s and 1960s most of Africa attained independent statehood.

The paradox is this. The word imperialism is said to character-ise the latter period just as it did the former. We hear as much of imperialism today as in the late nineteenth century. Clearly this suggests some major definitional problems. If imperialism is to be taken as referring to a specific phenomenon that occurs in international politics, then it follows from the contrast drawn above that the manifestations of this phenomenon are not the same for every historical period. But then, we may legitimately ask, if the face of imperialism can change so dramatically over such a short span of time, are we not begging the question by assuming that, beneath these various masks, there is an underly-ing reality, a persisting set of characteristics that gives meaning, identity and continuity to a concept of imperialism? And if there is not, are we not in fact talking about discrete historical pheno-mena rather than about one concept?

One way out of this problem is to view imperialism in the most general of terms as a recurrent relationship of control but allow-ing that the precise means by which this control is attained varies from historical period to period. Accordingly, a concept of impe-rialism might be developed along the following lines:

(1) First, there must be a disparity of power between the subject and the object of imperialism and this disparity must be one of kind rather than of degree. By which I mean that French annexations in Northern Africa were imperialism whereas the Franco-Prussian war of 1870 was not; Japanese policy in Manchuria was imperialism whereas the attack on Pearl Harbor was not.

(2) Secondly, imperialism suggests a relationship of control or the disposition to establish a relationship of control of one state or group over another. This distinguishes imperialism from other words in the vocabulary of international politics. It distinguishes it from colonialism or expansionism *per se* because those terms depend on a physical presence that need not be associated with imperialism. An imperialist relationship of control can be established by scarcely visible political, econ-omic and psychological pressures although it does not exclude a physical presence.

(3) Thirdly, the methods employed to exercise this control may vary, depending not on the motivation underlying the impe-

rialist drive but on objective external conditions that determine the forms that it is practicable for this control to take. By expressing the point this way we are doing more than seeking a definition that is wide enough to suit all historical contexts. It makes a substantive and a useful point. And that point is that there was no necessary connection between the nature of the imperial drive and the nature of specific imperialist techniques. To take an example. Even if we accept the validity of Hobson's thesis that imperialism was inspired by the search for investment outlets, what determined the fact that Africa was partitioned was not this ambition but rather various historical factors that made partition both possible and desirable. Given a different historical context, the desire to control may still have had its source in the search for investment opportunities but the desire could as easily have been fulfilled in another way – by non-annexationist means. Similarly, whatever motivation lies behind the desire to control in the present age, the fact that this desire is not expressed in annexationist terms is determined by the non-availability of territory for annexation or by the high political, economic or military costs involved in acquiring such territory.

How does this pertain to a discussion of spheres of influence? According to this conception of imperialism as a relationship of control, spheres of influence would be one technique for the maintenance of such control. Moreover, spheres of influence themselves have changed in precisely the same way as imperialism in general and can be used as an illustration of the point that although the imperialist urge to control is fairly constant, the specific manifestations of it vary from one historical period to another.

In other words, changes in the nature of spheres of influence have reflected the more general changes that have taken place in the nature of imperialistic control over the past century or so. As one analyst of spheres of influence has written

the formal agreements of the late 19th and early 20th centuries often preceded any actual influence and were intended to prevent or limit conflict which might occur between European powers as they expanded into Africa and Asia. In this respect, they are unlike contemporary spheres of influence. To the extent that contemporary spheres of in-

fluence have limited conflict, this has been an effect and not a cause of them.[30]

There was, then, a type of spheres-of-influence agreement that was appropriate to the annexationist phase of imperialism and now there is a new form of sphere of influence appropriate to the non-annexationist phase.

How would we define such a sphere? One writer has discerned three integral parts of the concept of a sphere of influence in post-1945 world politics and, although his formulation leaves some questions unanswered, they are worth reproducing at this stage. The three are: a declared interest of a power to achieve such a dominating status; recognition of this claim by other important members of the world community; and acquiescence of the local regimes or their resignation to a condition of dependency.[31]

The questions raised by the notion of spheres of influence all relate directly to issues of hierarchy. As our historical survey of the evolution of the international system has shown, there has been a perennial tendency to ascribe special rights to the Great Powers in accordance with their power status. The point about this is that some writers would argue that a hierarchical arrangement of states and an inegalitarian distribution of privileges within that hierarchy constitutes a valuable contribution to international order. As Hedley Bull has put it:

Because states are grossly unequal in power, certain international issues are as a consequence settled, the demands of certain states (weak ones) can in practice be left out of account, the demands of certain other states (strong ones) recognised to be the only ones relevant to the issue in hand ... The inequality of states in terms of power has the effect, in other words, of simplifying the pattern of international relations.[32]

Put crudely, this means that hierarchy enhances international order by avoiding recourse to war every time a dispute comes up: since we know in advance that a big power will defeat a small one, we can proceed directly to a solution of the dispute by simply letting the big power have its way.

Those analysts who see virtue in spheres of influence base their case on much the same kind of reasoning. They see spheres of influence as a positive contribution to international order in the sense that they serve to limit conflict between the Super-Powers and they do so by demarcating areas considered vital to the

respective Super-Powers and by stabilising each power's enjoyment of rights within its respective sphere. For instance, the USSR could invade Hungary and Czechoslovakia in 1956 and 1968 without any fear of reprisal from the West. Had these two states not fallen unequivocally within the Soviet sphere of influence, there might well have been a danger of serious conflict between the Super-Powers. But the existence of this sphere of influence and its recognition by the West effectively removed this area as a possible source of conflict between the rival Super-Powers.

This argument that spheres of influence contribute to international order by limiting the areas of competition between the major powers can be illustrated negatively by the case of the Cuban crisis in 1962. Essentially, the significance of the Cuban crisis was that it represented a Soviet attempt to change the boundaries of the American sphere of influence or, at least, amounted to a Soviet refusal to recognise the traditional contours of the American sphere. As a consequence, the world was pushed towards the brink of nuclear war. Spheres of influence, therefore, are thought to prevent confrontations of the Cuban kind – as long as both sides' spheres are mutually recognised.

There are several difficulties in coming to terms with spheres of influence and in assessing their place in the post-1945 international system. In the first instance, as was noted in a quotation above, their contribution to conflict-prevention is incidental to their primary role, which we have said is as an expression of the imperialist urge to control. Any assessment of spheres would be derelict if it did not take this into account.

Additionally, while spheres of influence may contribute to order by reducing the areas of rivalry between the Super-Powers, it surely has to be insisted that they undermine other constituents of international order. In any recounting of the principles upon which order has traditionally been based, sovereignty and non-intervention in domestic affairs would figure prominently and yet these are the principles that have most obviously been subordinated to the order sustained by spheres of influence.

Lastly, there is the problem of discerning in what sense spheres of influence are based upon conscious agreements or formally accepted rules of the game. To the extent that they are, they may

well be regarded as a form, albeit limited, of group norm of the kind that has underlain Great-Power Concert diplomacy of the past. Here, however, the basis of agreement appears too tenuous to support a working Concert system: Bull is undoubtedly correct when he states that 'Soviet-American spheres-of-influence understandings have so far been negative in content rather than positive'.[33] It was also argued in relation to the Concert of Europe that one of its operative rules was the requirement of 'formal consent'. Likewise, the attempt to build a post-1918 Concert was based on the formal rules of the covenant. In this sense, because spheres of influence are informal, there is difficulty in knowing their status in the eyes of the Super-Powers. Kaufman points out this problem when he notes that 'it is hard to establish that a mutual agreement does exist reciprocally legitimising the rule of the rival superpowers in their respective spheres of influence' but he lamely begs the issue, rather than resolves it, when he concludes that 'it seems most probable that an understanding does exist to a certain degree'.[34]

CRISIS MANAGEMENT AND 'DÉTENTE'

Can the 'conventions of crisis management' or the rules of détente provide a sufficiently coherent framework for Concert diplomacy in the post-1945 era, even if only a limited Concert of two Super-Powers? There is little reason to think so. In fact, as with some of the previous regulatory systems considered in this book, there is a suggestion that such rules of Super-Power relations as have been observed have been a product of the post-1945 order rather than the cause of it – a reflection of the specific balance of power rather than the conscious adherence to formalised precepts.

That this is so is amply revealed in the central ambiguity within the very concept of crisis management itself. On the one hand, the term has been used to denote the art of winning diplomatic victory: a crisis is 'managed' if the opponent is made to back down. On the other, crisis management has been used to refer to a set of practices whereby the Super-Powers 'ride' a crisis and consciously seek to avoid the outbreak of war between them. On the basis of this distinction, there is reason for believing that,

in their responses to crises, the respective Super-Powers have acted more often on the basis of a calculation of unilateral advantage than out of a concern for the universal good.

We might characterise the main difference between these two conceptions of crisis management as that between conflict-utilisation and conflict-avoidance. The distinction is amply summarised by P. Williams. He says of the former conception that

crises are not regarded as pathological or distasteful but rather as an opportunity for aggrandisement. It is the opposing state and not the crisis itself that is the enemy. Far from being a partnership, there is fierce competition or rivalry in which every attempt is made to manipulate or influence the adversary's behaviour in desired directions.

Of the latter, he observes that

implicit in this view is the notion of a crisis as a pathological occurrence to be ended or defused as quickly as possible. The aim is to control the situation and dampen down the conflict ... The crisis itself is the real enemy and the participants are actually partners in the task of eliminating the dangers of war and restoring things to normal.[35]

The vast majority of post-1945 crises have been managed in the former, rather than the latter, sense and have, therefore, been exercises in the balance of power rather than displays of a Super-Power Concert. Even in such cases where management of the latter kind seems to have occurred, there can be no assurance that the powers have been moved in their behaviour by acceptance of 'rules' and 'conventions' or whether the tactical demands of specific events have not produced a fortuitous convergence of interests.

The question as to whether the Super-Powers consciously adhere to crisis conventions is the crucial one and has been by no means resolved in favour of the theorists of crisis management. A useful example is provided in Coral Bell's seminal work.[36] In her discussion of the Quemoy crisis of 1958, she refers to American 'creative use of ambiguity' in its diplomatic signalling, whereby President Eisenhower and Secretary of State Dulles emitted two very different forms of signal. However, the reader is somewhat perplexed to be told that this 'diplomatic success' had been gained 'largely by a *conscious or unconscious* use of ambiguity'.[37] If the ambiguity was conscious, all is well and we can perhaps speak of crisis management (although for this to be regarded as a 'group

norm', it would also be necessary for the receivers of the ambiguous signals to appreciate their significance). If, however, the ambiguity was not conscious or intended, what we have instead is a typical piece of bureaucratic bungling with one voice of government saying one thing and another voice saying something else – diplomatic mismanagement rather than crisis management. The point about this example is that it is extremely difficult to tell whether the participants in a crisis are actually operating in accordance with a code of crisis etiquette or whether the academic analyst is merely reading such a code into behaviour that is random and undisciplined.

There is a further problem. By which criteria should we measure whether, and how successfully, crisis management has taken place? Do we assess it in terms of the interests of one of the Super-Powers, in terms of a common Super-Power interest in avoiding conflict or can we relate it to some wider notion of the interests of international society? For instance, the Super-Powers may manage a third-party crisis, such as that in the Middle East, so as to minimise hostilities but without necessarily settling the underlying issue of the crisis. Can we speak of 'management' in such a context? If crisis management is designed to avoid conflict rather than settle issues, should we necessarily assume that what is convenient for the Super-Powers is also in the best interests of the other members of international society?

One last comment on crisis management is worth making. In some of the literature, there is the not-unreasonable suggestion that, given the existence of nuclear weapons and the enormity of nuclear violence, crisis management can be regarded as a kind of functional substitute for actual war. In this case, as war can no longer be regarded as politically rational, but as the system still requires some mechanism for reaching political decisions, the management of the crisis and the diplomatic manouevring that accompanies it is the new means of resolving conflicts. If we push this interpretation to its ultimate conclusion, the powers involved in a crisis are in a quasi-war situation and playing for big stakes and it is scarcely conceivable that the 'game' would be played out according to neat and tidy gentlemen's rules. In other words, if the provenance of crisis conventions is a limited one, we should not have expected it to be otherwise.

There is some overlap between the notions of crisis management and détente, both having been seen as patterns in post-1945 Super-Power relations, with the major distinction being that détente has been a diplomatic technique for overall Super-Power relations rather than simply a code that is activated when crisis occurs. C. Bell's conception of détente is as 'a diplomatic strategy for a triangular power balance',[38] and she sees it as having been the dominant mode of managing the central balance since 1969.

How then should we locate the strategy of détente within our spectrum ranging from balance to Concert policies? Does détente signify a substantial modification of balance strategies as the Concert of Europe did, if only partially, and as the League attempted to do, but without success? Coral Bell's comments are instructive. Given the adversary context in which détente has arisen, and as with crisis management, Bell is insistent that 'it does not in any way imply an end to the contest for diplomatic influence, only a mode of making the contest less dangerous'.[39] She adds, and here we should recall the Concert of Europe, that 'Détente should certainly not be mistaken for peace. Peace is an objective, détente is a diplomatic mode or strategy by which that objective (or others) may be sought.'[40] Both of these statements, while not in themselves descriptive of détente as a Super-Power Concert, are at least fully compatible with such an interpretation.

However, Bell subsequently makes it clear that she does not regard détente as a set of Concert principles for the Super-Powers: 'Obviously a balance of power underlay the nineteenth-century concert of powers, or it would not have proved viable, just as a balance of power is now necessary as the foundation of the détente, which is not a concert of powers.'[41] The phraseology implies that such a concert may nonetheless be in the process of emergence although no indication is given as to how it will materialise. Indeed, in view of Bell's approving citation of Castlereagh's opinion that in a Concert system the powers feel a common duty as well as a common interest, one is left wondering what the source of this common duty will be perceived to be by the powers involved.

Is it then, appropriate to characterise the post-1945 order as a reversion to balance policies in which a Concert system has not simply failed but has not even been aspired to? It must be

conceded that the posing of the issue in these terms creates a genuine problem of interpretation and it may well be impossible to arrive at an assessment acceptable to all schools of thought.

On the one hand, we can be confident in our conclusion, which has been the thesis of this chapter, that the behaviour of the major powers, in their relations with each other, has not been sufficiently regulated by formally accepted rules for us to be able to speak of a functioning post-1945 Concert system. The reasons for such a conclusion have been cogently stated by Bull elsewhere but bear repetition at this point:

There has been no attempt to formalise a Soviet-American concert. There is no regular attempt to concert, in the sense of the holding of regular discussions concerned to define common and unique objectives, to map out a common strategy for attaining them and for distributing the burdens of such a strategy ... Nor has there been enunciated any theory or ideology of world order, such as underlay the Holy Alliance or the later European concert, that would give direction and purpose to a Soviet-American concert.[42]

On the other hand, if not as a Concert, how are we to characterise the Great-Power tutelage of the post-1945 order? The problem from this perspective is that many reasonable analysts have given weighty reasons why a description of post-war international politics in balance terminology would not be appropriate. Morse, for one, has roundly declaimed that 'the world simply does not conform to the patterns established in the Westphalian framework'[43] and that 'the balance of power has ceased to be useful as a description of the international system'.[44]

We can be sympathetic to this line of reasoning but reject its ultimate conclusion. Of course international politics are now vastly more complex than previously, with a host of new state actors, as well as many non-state ones, with a change of emphasis to new, and in many cases non-military, issues and with a greater degree of 'linkage' or 'interdependence' within the whole. This much must be readily conceded. Nonetheless, when we consider the ways in which the major international political processes have functioned, and the ways in which the Great Powers have related to each other, it is difficult to deny totally the validity of the balance concept. The conclusion that suggests itself, unsatisfactory as it might appear, is that until the balance system becomes

something else, it remains a balance system even if altered in form. As no one can adequately define what has taken the place of the previous system, and as we can be sure that it is not diplomacy by Concert, then the description of the post-1945 world as an age of balance is, perhaps, the least misleading of the alternatives.

Conclusion: full circle?

This book has been concerned with both ideas and practices in relation to international order and to its potential for reform. It can, however, provide little insight into. the mutual interaction between ideas and practices. That images of international order and historical patterns of international order affect each other is uncontroversial but trite: meanwhile, the precise nature of this inter-relationship resists adequate analysis.

Nor should we have expected otherwise. It has been noted in the course of this study that 'optimism' and 'pessimism', whether in relation to the need for international reform or the possibility of its attainment, have been persistent attitudes of mind. At the same time, one or other of these moods has tended to become dominant during various phases of history: we tend to associate some periods with a prevailing mood of optimism or pessimism and these moods fluctuate, if not in cyclical fashion, then at least at fairly regular intervals.

It is, of course, possible to discern why some intellectual moods do arise. Most obviously, fears and hopes about the nature of international order are generated by events in the real world of international politics, be it in the form of current experience, or recent memories, or imminent expectations. Dramatic events, such as wars, exercise the most profound influence but can, as we have seen, inspire hope even as they fill us with fear and despair. If the mood of the 1920s was one of confidence, then this was surely a product of the League experiment and the appearance, even if superficial, of a new order of international politics having been inaugurated, just as the despondency of the 1930s was associated with the highly visible failure of the League experiment and the seeming reversion to naked power politics: intellectually, a predominantly utopian temperament was superceded by a predominantly realist one. Similarly, it could be argued that, as far as the climate of international politics was concerned, nuclear weaponry cast a more gloomy shadow over the 1950s than over the 1960s if for no other reason than the

growing to maturity of a generation that, in the cliché, has learned to live with the bomb. The student of the 1970s who opens Inis Claude's impressive *Power and International Relations*, written at the height of the Cold War, cannot fail to detect a slightly alien mood in the stark and sombre opening passages to the effect that 'mankind stands in grave danger of irreparable self-mutilation or substantial self-destruction' and that 'the march of military technology is so rapid that it is no longer premature to contemplate the danger of the annihilation of the human race'.[1] The possibility of such an occurrence has not lessened in the interval but the seeming durability of the 'nuclear peace' has fostered its own acceptance.

At the same time, moods of optimism and pessimism appear also to have their sources in a type of theoretical speculation that may itself be divorced from the current practice of international politics. The realist reorientation within the academic discipline of international politics, which established itself during the 1940s, was as much a reaction to the theoretical inadequacies of the previous generation of writers as it was to the specific international events of the 1930s. We could also insist that there was no very obvious diversity in historical experience to account for the differing temperaments of Rousseau and Kant. In other words, the very moods of those who think seriously about the nature and patterns of international order appear to derive from a mixture of practical and theoretical concerns.

There is a further difficulty in attempting to relate practices to ideas in the history of international order. In this historical survey, a recurring theme of analytic interest has been the effects, in terms of peace or stability, of the application of specific 'norms' of inter-state behaviour. At the most general level, it has been asked implicitly in the foregoing discussion whether 'Concert' or 'balance' practices tend to be more beneficial in their contribution to international order and it should already be clear that no satisfactory answer can be given to this question.

The problem that we started out with, which has not been resolved, is whether various kinds of international norms are creative of specific conditions of peace and stability or whether, conversely, it is the prior existence of conditions of stability that facilitates the adoption of co-operative norms. Did the norms of

Concert diplomacy create the peace of 1815–54 or was the Concert parasitic upon the peace? Likewise, did the League produce the peace of the 1920s or did the peace of the 1920s create the illusion of an effective League system? Is its impotence revealed by its inability to cope with the real problems that arose in the 1930s? Is the post-1945 peace attributable to the rules of nuclear deterrence and the conventions of crisis management or have these norms been adopted because other factors rendered them acceptable?

If ideas about international order are not themselves 'independent variables', and if the effects of specific attempts to apply norms of international order are themselves so uncertain, then it is surely fair to conclude that the inter-relationship between ideas and practices is a complex one in which it is impossible to analyse how images of desirable international orders come to be, or fail to be, turned into reality. The proposition of one writer who contends that ideas and practices may be mutually reinforcing– in a progressive direction – is, accordingly, over-simple. His argument is as follows:

The view that there is indeed progress is thus capable of generating a circle of mutually supporting arguments in the ideology of the society of international relations theorists: there is an order in international society which can be understood; if we understand we are better able to control and direct; the ability to control and direct allows us to cause improvements, which, in time, confirm our improving and understanding of international society.[2]

Were we all optimists, this might well be so. However, the circle of pessimistic thought is equally self-perpetuating and the real world reflects the tensions of the two competing claims.

There have been some persistent themes in this diplomatic story. At one level, the history of the period from 1815 can be seen as a series of attempts to instil a measure of order into international life. In the first half of the nineteenth century this was done by means of a combination of the techniques of the balance of power with the techniques of the Concert of Europe. In the second half of the century, there was a reversion to the techniques of the balance of power expressed in a highly formalised system of alliances. In the period 1919–39, the powers employed the new

diplomatic device of the League of Nations coupled with traditional means for the assurance of national security. In the period
after 1945, order has been maintained, formally by the United
Nations, informally and more effectively by a balance between
two highly integrated and antagonistic blocs.

In a sense then, at this level, the story appears almost as a
continuing effort on the part of states to divest themselves of their
more basic nature and to organise international life on the basis
of a more lofty ideal. And at this level, the story is then one of
varying degrees of failure.

Such a judgement may, however, be tempered. From which
perspective – chronological or cultural – are we to pass judgement upon the evolving international order and upon the condition of the present order? How are we to assess the attainment
of progress or its absence as it affects international political
arrangements?

The question of perspective is worth dwelling upon. Let us
consider, first, the chronological perspective. In attempting to
measure the degree and direction of change within the international polity since 1815, which time-span is the appropriate
one? Certainly, we can agree that some historical perspective is
necessary in order to visualise elements of both continuity and
change. As Stanley Hoffmann has reminded us, berating studies
that focus exclusively on the present:

> Because we have an inadequate basis for comparison, we are tempted to
> exaggerate either continuity with a past that we know badly, or the
> radical originality of the present, depending on whether we are more
> struck by the features we deem permanent, or with those we do not
> believe existed before. And yet a more rigorous examination of the past
> might reveal that what we sense as new really is not, and that some of
> the 'traditional' features are far more complex than we think.[3]

Agreement that a historical perspective is needed does not,
unfortunately, lead to agreement as to *which* historical perspective. In this study, we have sought for patterns of international order within the 1815–1980 period. Could this time-
frame be over-restrictive? If we consider a book such as
Bozeman's *Politics and Culture in International History*, the fact is
impressed upon us that the modern European state system, with
its principal characteristics, is only one variant form of organi-

sation in the relationships between individual cultures and political systems.[4] Consequently, to look for minor modifications in patterns of international order within a short period of the modern state system (even when the system is, as now, writ large) may be to do violence to a genuinely world-historic perspective and blind us to the realisation that there are alternative systems of order between peoples, apart from the modification of rules and norms within a clearly established and continuing system.

Secondly, in passing judgement upon the need for change, and the degree of its attainment, we have also to give consideration to the question of which perspective – cultural or geographical – is the appropriate one. To adapt a worn aphorism, where one stands in one's assessment of the current international order will depend crucially upon where one sits. To make only the most obvious of points, in the recent words of Oran Young, 'it is hardly surprising that those who live in wealthy countries tend to be more complacent about the performance of the international polity than those who live in poor countries'.[5] International orders are not neutral in their consequences for national societies; some states benefit more from certain international arrangements than do others. It follows, therefore, that we cannot expect consensus upon the need for reform or about the direction reform should take. As Richard Falk has expressed it 'the unevenness of the struggle for global reform – what is right for most Latin American, Asian, and African countries is not the same as what is right for the Trilateral countries of Japan, Western Europe, or North America, or for the Soviet Bloc countries – makes it impossible to provide global generalizations'.[6]

Culturally, it is probably also true that the dominant institutions and characteristics of present international order are more likely to be mistaken as the only form of order by Europeans, or westerners generally, because that order is mainly their creation, the fruit of a predominantly western political tradition. Bozeman has articulated this perspective at some length and may be quoted in this context:

The complex framework of international organizations that spans the world today may thus be viewed as the logical culmination of the political history of the West. As a nonterritorial power structure ... it recalls the traditions set by the great medieval concerts. As an in-

ternational extension of the modern democratic state it incorporates the values that have governed European and American societies in recent centuries.[7]

Bearing these caveats in mind, how might we then assess the present international order and the extent of change or progress since 1815? Overall, it is difficult to detect any major restructuring of the operative principles of international politics. To put it in its simplest terms, a Talleyrand or Metternich reincarnated at the present time would have little difficulty in mastering the rules of the international political game. As one analyst has argued:

The dramatic changes that have occurred in world society in the last few decades have not included among them such a revolutionary transformation of the international political structure ... The state system – the ultimate cause of war – remains. The problem of security is still present. The role of force and the threat of it have thus not been eliminated. Strategic considerations and the traditional meaning of power still have relevance.[8]

Clearly, therefore, the system of international politics continues to be a system of interaction between sovereign, independent states and at this level, the international order has evidently not been reformed in any meaningful way. Indeed, some would have it that the persistence of this system ensures that no substantial reform can ever take place. This is the thrust of von Geusau's complaint:

In structural and organizational terms the European concept of the sovereign national state offers no perspectives on world order. The system of diplomacy built upon this concept has proved to be a barrier to, instead of a channel for, world order. Diplomatic representation promotes attitudes of defending abstract and divisive national interests, when concern for human suffering and protection of life would have been necessary ... It is concerned with the status and prestige of an abstract entity, rather than the hunger, the torture or the fear of real men.[9]

Even if the system, in structural terms, has not changed, it would nonetheless be possible for some of its norms to have developed and to have demonstrated progress, whether in content or in degree of general acceptance. Can we demonstrate significant changes in the nature of these norms? Little evidence is forthcoming in support of such a proposition. When we recall that the system of nuclear deterrence is an important component

of the present international order, and when one analyst can specify the ground-rules of the 'nuclear regime' as being those of 'anarchy', 'equilibrium' and 'hierarchy',[10] we can be forgiven for assuming that the essentials of a balance system remain with us. In fact, implicit in the many studies seeking to correlate system stability with the degree of system polarity is a logic of numbers equally applicable to the post-1945 period as it is to the eighteenth and nineteenth centuries. Such logic must surely be based on the assumption that basic norms have not changed throughout this period, even though there have been changes in the number of 'poles' and major changes in the nature of military technology.[11]

Others would even argue that, in terms of co-operative international norms, far from there being progress since 1815, there has been observable regress. Luard makes precisely such a point when he refers to the eclipse of Concert norms in the current international situation. Luard draws the comparison between nineteenth-century international politics and present practices and reaches the following judgement. 'For all the concern of nationalism to build powerful and independent states, the collective principle established by the Concert meant that states became more accountable to others for their behaviour than ever before: they were indeed more so than they are today.'[12]

Thus far, we have been mainly concerned with the political apparatus and decision-making norms of international society. What deserves to be pointed out is that the economic dimensions of international order are becoming a focus of increasing attention and that any assessment of progress in relation to the evolution of the international system would be inadequate if it did not take into account its economic aspects. In part, this is so because of the new-found awareness of the interaction of the global system's political and economic structures and the realisation that the differential impact of various international orders is nowhere more apparent than in the distribution of economic benefits. It follows, therefore, that the present calls for a new international economic order, based as they are upon the view of the integral union between power-political influence and prevailing economic structures, have broadened out the agenda of international-order reform and that this, as in other areas, has

partially been in response to the poor performance of the current order as a means of economic distribution. If we therefore incorporate this economic dimension into our conception of the evolving international order, we would be led to a correspondingly pessimistic judgement. Oran Young, while arriving at an otherwise generally favourable assessment of the performance of the international polity, concedes that it is open to censure on this score at least:

Many inequalities in the international polity have exhibited a marked tendency to become more extreme rather than less extreme during modern times. With respect to material wealth, for example, this trend has been dramatic over the last hundred years. Thus, it is not possible to sound an optimistic note in this realm by suggesting that there is at least a trend toward greater equality in the distribution of values.[13]

In other words, if equality is one of our measures of progress, then in relation to the international economic order, which can scarcely be separated from the workings of the whole, progress has thus far remained elusive.

Another theme running through the past century-and-a-half of international experience is that of conflict between the interests of the small powers and the interests of the greater powers. This was an issue that was first raised explicitly in connection with the congress system in as much as that system appeared to be a flagrant example of the Great Powers running the international show with scant respect for the interests of the small states. In their settlements, the Great Powers casually determined the fate of the lesser states on no principle other than their own convenience. It was to be likewise with the alliance systems at the end of the century. It was the Great Powers that were involved in the alliances and it was the smaller states, and also the colonial territories, that were employed as mere objects for changing or restoring the balance between these great powers.

The dispute between the smaller and the greater powers was to be opened again in relation to the drafting of both the Covenant of the League and the Charter of the United Nations. The former gave the major role to the Great Powers but made substantial concessions to the other states both in the Assembly of the League and in the Council. By way of contrast, the United Nations Charter, much more forcefully than the covenant, asserted the special role of the Great Powers in international affairs.

There is something paradoxical about this. It is a fairly conventional view that in some sense the effort to establish international organisations represents the expression of the aspiration towards an improved international order. If this is so, and if there has been any progress from the days of the Concert of Europe to the establishment of the United Nations, then it would be reasonable to suppose that the UN represents the ethical ideals of international relations as they have developed over the past couple of centuries. At the same time, it is frequently stated that one of the most ethically abhorrent aspects of international relations has been this perpetual dominance of the Great Powers over the lesser members of the international system. Certainly this was one of Woodrow Wilson's major complaints about the traditional system of power politics. But if the UN represents the progress of ideas about a more equitable international society, then on this precise question of the relationship between, and the relative powers of, the great and small states, there would seem to have been no progress whatsoever. In fact, the UN in its original conception represented a quite definite return to the days of the congress system and refused to make even those concessions to small-power opinion that had been made in the League covenant.

What, then are we to make of this apparent paradox? There are at least two views that we might take of it – the 'whig' and the 'tory' interpretations respectively.

According to the whig account, the lack of progress on the issue of constructing a more egalitarian international order would˗ be explained by the deceit and cunning of the Great Powers themselves. Butterfield noted of the whig interpretation that through its 'system of immediate reference to the present-day, historical personages can easily and irresistibly be classed into the men who furthered progress and the men who tried to hinder it'.[14] That is to say that history is populated by heroes and villains. At the international level it is the Great Powers themselves who are the villains: there has been no diminution of the hierarchical aspects of international order because the Great Powers did not desire any and because they had the means to prevent any 'progressive' developments on this issue.

There is another view that could be regarded as the tory interpretation. According to this, the drafters of the Charter had

a clearer perception of the realities of international order than did Wilson and his contemporaries. They realised that international order would be made more, not less, stable by emphasising hierarchical arrangements and not by attempting to eliminate them. No ethical sentiment or egalitarian impulse can change the fact that some states are inherently more powerful than others and that these Great Powers, if thwarted in their vital interests, can do much more damage to international order than can dissatisfied small states. It was in this connection that some have argued that the doctrine of formal equality, at the international level, represents 'a spurious application of a nominally democratic principle to the unsuitable environment of international relations'. Vincent continues:

Thus, in regard to the United Nations, it might be argued that the doctrine of one-state-one-vote that follows from the principle of equality gets in the way of the efficient working of the organization. It does so by preventing the writ of the powerful, on whose support the survival of the organization depends, from running and by allowing resolutions to be carried by coalitions of small states of whose acceptance in the international community at large there is little prospect.[15]

In short, the attempt to give institutional expression to a basic equality among states is, in any case, misconceived and we should not bemoan the lack of 'progress' in that direction.

Anyone who studies the recent development of the international political system cannot fail to be struck by another evident paradox. If we concede, as we surely must, that the performance of the international order has been deficient in many respects, and if we also conclude that there has been little change in the nature of that order, is there not something puzzling in the manner in which this inefficient polity has tenaciously maintained its basic characteristics? The extent of this puzzle depends, of course, on how deficient one assumes the system to have been but even Oran Young's relative equanimity, as noted above, does not conceal this puzzle from him. He is led to observe that 'the international polity constitutes a curious case in which a rather poor performance record along other dimensions is coupled with an impressive exhibit of durability'.[16] Arguably, the international political system has experienced less change in its central struc-

tures and its operating norms than any other political system that has functioned during the period since 1815.

Why should this be? There is a simple answer to this question which appears to satisfy but on reflection gives rise to a series of consequent questions. It has been provided, amongst others, by P. Savigear and its initial premise is that international politics are no more than the untidy fringes of domestic politics and, as such, are not susceptible to the same progressive developments as have occurred within states. Savigear explains why the philosophy of international relations has remained static while political philosophy generally has been dynamic:

> The state has changed – the precise form of that change may be in dispute, some would say from dynastic to absolutist and to democratic for example – and the philosophy of the state has changed with it. Thought about International Relations, and indeed International Relations themselves, have not so changed ... There is not the same sense of moving forward through the history of thought that characterizes the traditional presentation of political theory because in a way there *was* a progression in the changing nature of the relationship between ruler and ruled ... The conception of the state was thus eroded from within by the theorists of the internal ordering of the state, but this did not happen for those writers who drew their arguments about International Relations from political philosophy.[17]

Put simply, international politics is about the relationships between states, regardless of the nature of the states themselves, and changes in patterns of domestic order do not, in turn, lead to new patterns of international order.

As a characterisation of the theory of international relations this, as will be argued below, is a half-truth. Before pursuing this issue, however, it is worth asking why there should be this disjunction in thought between internal order and international order. Why, in the course of the past two centuries, have all domestic political systems been faced with, and acceded to, demands for major restructuring while the international polity has remained obdurate to pressures for change? Could the tentative answer be that people have expected much less from the international system? This, in turn, is explicable in terms of the inability of people to discern readily how the international system benefits them or harms them: their demands are directed at, and their wants are assumed to be satisfied by, domestic polities. The

effects of the international system upon individual lives are, as a generalisation, but dimly perceived beyond the names of dead soldiers on countless local cenotaphs.

It is worth observing that, if the theorists of 'complex interdependence' are correct, then this situation may be changing and the international polity may become the focal point of increasing demands. As people come to recognise the impotence of individual governments, primarily but not exclusively in economic terms, they will more consciously direct attention to the nature of international order and seek satisfaction in that quarter. The appeals for a new international economic order may illustrate this trend to the extent that they are based on a recognition of the fact that individual third-world governments cannot deliver 'development' without some adjustment of the world's economic system.

As mentioned above, the theory of inter-state relationships appears to have been static, in spite of the many changes that have taken place within the state itself. The implication of this is that there is no such thing as a 'progressive' theory of international relations. Are we to accept this as a valid characterisation of theoretical speculation in the field of international politics?

In one sense, there is some truth in this proposition. In terms of 'progressive' international theories, we have already confronted such a doctrine in the shape of the Kantian model of international change. However, we would surely have to concede that, although optimistic in its ultimate prognosis about the future international order and although firmly grounded on a theory of progress, the Kantian model remains a fearsome and distressing one. The view has been expressed that 'history does not move forward without catastrophe'.[18] This, like the Kantian, is a theory of progress but the manner of its attainment casts its own depressing shadow.

Were the Kantian vision the only progressive theory of international relations, there might well be grounds for saying that no genuine theory of international progress exists. However, there are other bodies of ideas which deserve consideration in this context: functionalism, liberal–democratic 'internationalism' and the general Marxist–Leninist tradition all contain within them

theories of international progress. A brief comment may be made on each.

Functionalism may be viewed as one of the major peace theories of the twentieth century, although many of its intellectual components stretch back at least into the eighteenth century. Its classic formulation is to be found in Mitrany's *A Working Peace System.* The body of ideas associated with functionalism was, like the internationalist idealism of Woodrow Wilson, a reformist ideology – a prescription for improving the world and especially for eliminating violence at the international level. Unlike Wilsonian idealism, however, advocates of functionalism were suspicious about efforts to attain peace by the mere construction of international organisations such as the League. In fact, the functionalist creed represented an alternative to the more traditional efforts at ensuring peace in that it explicitly disavowed such facile constitutional–institutional solutions to the problems of international order.

The central concept in functionalism is that of basic human needs and its contention is that human loyalties will be directed toward the source of the fulfilment of these needs. While the state has traditionally been viewed in this role of 'provider', there are now important areas of human needs that, far from being furthered by the state, are positively thwarted by the existence of separate national jurisdictions. As these needs come to be fulfilled outside the state, so will loyalties come to be redirected towards new supra-national organisations. Unlike constitutional solutions to international order, functionalism does not advocate a direct challenge to the national sovereignty of the state: rather it expects that eventually, in the face of extending functional co-operation across national boundaries, these boundaries will become of decreasing political relevance. As with Marxism, functionalism presents an essentially materialist view of historical development and argues that, as a consequence of changes in the ways in which needs are satisfied, there will be corresponding changes in the international political superstructure. To some extent, as with traditional Marxism, the state will simply wither away. In this sense, functionalism constitutes an important instance of a theory of international progress.

A second such 'progressive' school is that represented by

liberal–democratic internationalism, a set of beliefs that was most clearly influential in the early years of the present century. Its intellectual force derived from its adoption of many liberal–democratic beliefs and assumptions of the nineteenth century and from its attempt to apply them in a different context – as having an applicability to international politics and not simply to internal politics.

The central pillar of this doctrine was the beneficial role of 'public opinion'. Broadly speaking, there were two reasons why the liberal internationalists wished to foster a greater role for public opinion in international affairs. The first of these was the increasingly 'democratic' nature of warfare itself: the experience of the First World War and its widespread slaughter, its far greater impact upon civilian populations and the tentative beginnings of airpower – all of these technological aspects of warfare had the common effect of ensuring that war would make itself felt within much wider sections of society than had hitherto been the case. Moreover, since warfare was likely to be universal in its effects, the democratic 'progressives' believed it only right that the public at large should be more intimately involved in the processes of international politics in order to try to prevent wars. In other words, while war was the sport of princes, it may have been permissible to leave diplomacy to the princes' close advisers but now that war was impinging more directly upon each and every life, the public at large was entitled to be consulted.

The second reason why the liberal internationalists emphasised the role of public opinion was a reflection of their faith in the inherent good sense of that opinion and of their faith that public opinion would act as a restraint upon the belligerent policies pursued by autocratic states. In this sense, we are back with Kant's proposition that a 'republican constitution' would be the best guarantee of peace. The belief rests upon two assumptions: that only in a democratic system will governmental representatives be accountable to, and controlled by, the people: and that because of the inherent moral good sense of the people, they will not permit their governments to pursue unscrupulous or warlike policies. Woodrow Wilson was a foremost champion of this position:

No nation is admitted to the League of Nations that cannot show that it has institutions which we call free ... Nobody is admitted except the self-governing nations, because it was the instinctive judgement of every man who sat around that board that only a nation whose government was its servant and not its master could be trusted to preserve the peace of the world.[19]

Even more succinctly, he contended that

a steadfast concert for peace can never be maintained except by a partnership of democratic nations. No autocratic government could be trusted to keep faith with it or observe its covenants.

Liberal internationalism was, therefore, another example of a progressive doctrine. It held to the position that the international order would be improved as a concomitant of the internal processes of democratisation that were occurring within states. Democratically constituted states would yield a peaceful and harmonious international order, without need for any further adjustment to international political structures.

Thirdly, and lastly, Marxism–Leninism may be said to embody a theory of international progress. It has often been observed that orthodox Marxism lacks any explicit theory of international relations whatsoever. This is not the place to enter into such a debate. Suffice it for present purposes to note that Marxist theory in general, because of its exposition of a series of sequential historical stages, is inherently 'progressive'. Each stage, for Marx, in some important sense marks an improvement upon the stage that preceded it. Moreover, progressive development is ensured by the dialectics of history. Finally, of course, the process culminates in the achievement of a communist society.

As far as international politics are concerned, the relevance of the Marxist–Leninist tradition may be confined to the following observation. In as much as international competition and the outbreak of wars are to be explained in terms of the contradictions of the capitalist system, then the resolution of these conflicts in the attainment of communist society will also resolve international conflict. If not explicit in Marxist theory, it is at least implicit, that the achievement of communist society would lead to major international restructuring, if for no other reason than the withering-away of the class-based state.

There are, of course, differences in the nature of the 'progress' postulated in these theories, and we might, with Paul Taylor, distinguish between 'episodic' and 'evolutionary' progress. In Taylor's analysis, the League of Nations was to constitute 'episodic' progress:

The fourteen points were very much in the tradition of the Lockean social contract; there was to be a single stage transition from a period of disgrace in which diplomacy was private and evil in its effects to a period of grace in which diplomacy would be open, democratic, and just. Progress in international society was thought to have a beginning and an end: it had to begin in present deficiencies and would finish on a kind of eternal plateau populated with contented and benign states.[20]

Such conceptions have tended to be superceded by 'evolutionary' notions:

That approach to the problems of world order called Functionalism is also more evolutionary than episodic; it stresses the ongoing and adaptive processes of international integration rather than a particular condition of integration.[21]

The three doctrines briefly discussed may, nonetheless, be taken as examples of 'progressive' international theories. However, in support of Savigear's observation that theories of international relations have not developed in the same way as have theories of the state itself, it might be legitimately objected that none of these three doctrines constitutes a theory of *autonomous* international progress. They are all derivative in as much as the progress that is prescribed for the international order is, in each case, parasitic upon internal domestic changes in the nature of the state. Once again, it may be argued that just as international politics emerged as a side-effect of the modern nation–state, so our theories of international progress are equally 'dependent' and we might see any restructuring of the international order to be contingent upon changes in the state units themselves.

Certainly, in each of the three bodies of theory we have considered, changes to the international order can be seen to be derivative from changes to the internal order within states, whether it be by the democratisation of the state or its gradual withering from within. This leads us to the important issue of the relationship between international order and internal domestic order and we might

observe that, even if international order is something more than the sum of domestic orders, it remains true that the two cannot be divorced from each other. In other words, it is impossible to visualise any form of satisfactory international order, however one might want to define it, that is not itself constructed upon satisfactory domestic orders.

This expresses the point rather abstractly and it may clarify matters to provide some examples. We have already referred to the prominent position of economic demands by third-world countries in present debates about the nature of a desirable international order. The point is simply that such demands for overall restructuring of the economic order would be pointless on their own if they were not taken in conjunction with measures to effect economic redistribution within individual third-world countries. This is not to take sides in the debate as to where the true causes of world poverty are to be located but, less ambitiously, to emphasise the uncontentious fact that the two dimensions of the problem, external and internal, are inter-related.[22] In short, a more equitable international order would not by itself suffice to ensure the improvement of the economic lot of the poorest sections of the world's population.[23]

Such an analysis is identical with that found within the school of Wilsonian internationalism discussed above. Its fundamental premise is that a stable international political order can only be achieved in unison with the creation of the domestic democratic orders necessary to sustain it.

One last point remains to be made. The principal theme of the book has been the various ways in which states have sought to manage the relations between them and this can mostly be reduced to a wavering between balance-of-power operations and a more highly organised Concert system. The consensus about the present international order seems to be that if the system is not yet operating as a multipolar balance, then this is at least the general trend of development: the five-power constellation envisaged by President Nixon and Henry Kissinger, whatever the difficulties with such a conception, cannot be totally dismissed. If this is an accurate depiction of the current situation, we have come full circle since the operations of the five-power balance as it emerged from the Congress of Vienna in 1815.

Whatever the precise configuration that characterises the present system, there can be little doubt that its basic operative principles derive from the balance-of-power model. As George Liska has recently written in the foreword to a book, comparing it with a study he had written some twenty years previously: 'Whereas the early effort dealt with international organization of collective security and stressed the smaller powers, the present one emphasizes great states involved in the balances of land- and sea-based power in the raw.'[24]

Throughout the period under review, the irreducible minimum that the states have had between them by way of a regulatory mechanism has been the balance of power. If the present system is no more than a balance one, then it would appear that the search over the past one-and-a-half centuries for a more highly developed form of international order has, at least temporarily, come to a halt.

Instead, the states appear to see virtue in the resurrection of the old balance system, perhaps of the eighteenth century, because they seem little disposed towards the elaboration of Concert diplomacy. What is important, and in a sense striking, is that statesmen are openly declaring that, in the present circumstances, the best means of maintaining international order is on the basis of the primitive model of the balance of power. For those who seek for progress, this is a dismal note on which to conclude. As Alaister Buchan has lamented, 'it would be a sorry world and one that risked alienating not only the lesser powers but our own younger generation as well if they were asked to believe that a balance of power is the highest political achievement of which the new great powers are capable'.[25]

The conclusion may be doubly dismal. We may readily acknowledge that, since 1815, we have come full circle. The thought may not inspire us but it is one that we can live with. What is more provocative is the realisation that, in the meantime, other variants of international order have been attempted and found wanting. What the present age lacks is any widely-shared vision of the direction that future reform should take. The question that lingers is, should the balance system prove defective for our future needs, where do we go from here?

Notes

INTRODUCTION: THE 'WHIG' AND 'TORY' INTERPRETATIONS

1   F. Meinecke, *Machiavellism*, English translation (Routledge and Kegan Paul, 1957).
2   For a discussion of 'Regulative Forces' see R. Rosecrance, *International Relations: Peace or War?* (McGraw Hill, 1973), ch. 5.
3   A. James, 'Law and Order in International Society' in A. James (ed.), *The Bases of International Order* (O.U.P., 1973), p. 61.
4   *Ibid.* p. 61.
5   *Ibid.* p. 63.
6   K. Waltz, 'Theory of International Relations', in F. Greenstein and N. Polsby (eds.), *International Politics*, Handbook of Political Science, vol. 8 (Addison-Wesley, 1975), pp. 39–40.
7   R. Keohane and J. Nye, *Power and Interdependence* (Little, Brown and Co., 1977), p. 21.
8   A. L. Burns, *Of Powers and Their Politics* (Prentice-Hall, 1968), p. 266.
9   *The Whig Interpretation of History* (Bell Edition, 1950), p. v.
10 *Ibid.* p. 12.
11 C. Van Doren, *The Idea of Progress* (Praeger, 1967), p. 3.
12 *Ibid.* pp. 373–4.
13 F. H. Hinsley, *Power and the Pursuit of Peace* (C.U.P., 1963), p. 13.
14 S. G. Goodspeed, *The Nature and Function of International Organisation*, 2nd ed. (O.U.P., 1967), p. 670.
15 H. Kohn, *World Order in Historical Perspective* (Harvard, 1942), p. 270.
16 *Ibid.* p. 279.
17 D. C. O'Brien, 'Modernisation, Order and the Erosion of a Democratic Ideal', *Journal of Development Studies*, 8, no. 4 (1972), 353.
18 Quoted in W. Camp, *The Glittering Prizes* (MacGibbon and Kee, 1960), p. 216.
19 G. Schwarzenberger, *Power Politics*, 3rd ed. (Stevens and Son, 1964), Part Two.
20 H. Bull, *The Anarchical Society: A Study of Order in World Politics* (Macmillan, 1977), p. 239.
21 *Swords Into Plowshares: The Problems and Progress of International Organisation* (University of London, 1965), p. 14.
22 S. Hoffmann, 'Rousseau on War and Peace', *American Political Science Review* (June 1963), 333.

1   INTERNATIONAL POLITICS AND THE PROBLEM OF ORDER

1   See the general introduction in R. Falk and S. Mendlovitz, *Regional Politics and World Order* (Freeman and Co., 1973), p. 6.
2   A. Rapoport in his introduction to Clausewitz, *On War* (Penguin edition, 1968).
3   H. Bull, 'Society and Anarchy in International Relations', in H. Butterfield and M. Wight (eds.), *Diplomatic Investigations* (Allen and Unwin, 1966), p. 35.
4   G. Modelski, 'World Order-Keeping' in G. Goodwin and A. Linklater (eds.), *New Dimensions of World Politics* (Croom Helm, 1975), p. 54.

2   KANT AND THE TRADITION OF OPTIMISM

1   *After Utopia: the decline of political faith* (Princeton University Press, 1957), p. vii.
2   'Practical International Futures' in A. Somit (ed.), *Political Science and the Study of the Future* (Dryden Press, 1974), pp. 286–7.
3   Some of the burgeoning literature will be cited in the course of this chapter. Details of the specific output of the World Order Models Project can be found in the recent review articles by Harold D. Lasswell, 'The Promise of the World Order Modelling Movement', *World Politics*, 29, no. 3 (April 1977), 425–37, and (from a critical perspective) by Tom Farer, 'The Greening of the Globe: a Preliminary Appraisal of the World Order Models Project (WOMP),' *International Organization* (winter 1977), 129–47.
4   Hinsley, *Power and Pursuit of Peace*, p. 3.
5   This classification is used by L. R. Beres and H. R. Targ (eds.), *Planning Alternative World Futures* (Praeger, 1975), pp. xiv–xv.
6   R. W. Cox, 'On Thinking about Future World Order', *World Politics*, 28, no. 2 (January 1976). Cox specifies three paradigmatic approaches to future world order: the natural–rational; the positivist–evolutionary; the historicist–dialectical.
7   *Ibid.* pp. 177–8.
8   J. Camilleri, *Civilization in Crisis: Human Prospects in a Changing World* (C.U.P., 1976), p. 183.
9   'The Theory of International Politics 1919–69' in B. Porter (ed.), *The Aberystwyth Papers* (O.U.P., 1972), p. 34.
10   Karl Mannheim, *Ideology and Utopia* (Routledge, 1960), p. 179.
11   This point is discussed in E. H. Carr, *The Twenty Years' Crisis* (Harper edition, 1964), Parts One and Two.
12   G. Evans, 'Some Problems with a History of Thought in International Relations', *International Relations*, 4, no. 6 (November 1974), 720.
13   J. Bentham, *Plan for an Universal and Perpetual Peace* (Grotius Society, 1927), p. 43.

14 *The Way of Peace* (Kennikat, 1968, original ed. 1928), p. 138.
15 See Carr, *Twenty Years' Crisis*, ch. 4.
16 A. E. Zimmern, 'The Future of Civilization' in R. Bourne (ed.), *Towards an Enduring Peace* (American Association for International Conciliation, 1916), p. 226.
17 Beres and Targ, *Alternative World Futures*, p. xvii.
18 See S. H. Mendlovitz's general introduction to 'Preferred Worlds for the 1990's', the series of WOMP studies.
19 *This Endangered Planet* (Vintage Books, 1971), p. 9.
20 *Civilization in Crisis*, p. 180.
21 The distinction between these two terms is discussed in Bull, *Anarchical Society*, pp. 8–22.
22 S. Rosen and W. Jones, *The Logic of International Relations*, 2nd ed. (Winthrop, 1977), p. 415.
23 J. D. Armstrong, 'Beyond the States System: Recent Conceptions of Future World Society', unpublished paper, Department of International Relations, Australian National University (August 1975), p. 1.
24 Cox, 'Future World Order', pp. 178–80.
25 C. F. von Weizacker, 'A Sceptical Contribution' in S. H. Mendlovitz (ed.), *On the Creation of a Just World Order*. Preferred Worlds for the 1990's (The Free Press, 1975), p. 114.
26 Farer, 'The Greening of the Globe', p. 132.
27 See Hinsley, *Power and Pursuit of Peace*, chs. 1 and 2.
28 Farer, 'The Greening of the Globe', p. 132.
29 See e.g. Hinsley, *Power and Pursuit of Peace*, ch. 4; K. Waltz, 'Kant, Liberalism and War', *American Political Science Review*, 56 (June 1962).
30 M. G. Forsyth, H. M. A. Keens–Soper and P. Savigear (eds.), *The Theory of International Relations* (Allen and Unwin, 1970), p. 211. All quotations from Kant are taken from the selections of his writings reproduced in this book.
31 *Ibid*. p. 220.
32 *Ibid*. p. 183.
33 *Ibid*. p. 213.
34 *Ibid*.
35 *International Relations*, p. 198.
36 *Ibid*. p. 194.
37 *Ibid*. pp. 194–5.
38 *Ibid*. p. 185.
39 *Ibid*. pp. 183–5.
40 Cited in Rosen and Jones, *International Relations*, p. 429.
41 L. R. Beres, 'Behavioural Paths to a new World Order' in Beres and Targ, *Alternative World Futures*, p. 273.
42 Falk draws attention to the same three reformist reactions in *This Endangered Planet*, pp. 283–4.

43 Quoted in K. Thompson, *Political Realism and the Crisis of World Politics* (Princeton University Press, 1960), p. 28.
44 Carr, *Twenty Years' Crisis*, p. 8.
45 E. Harris, *Annihilation and Utopia* (Allen and Unwin, 1966).
46 'The Constitutional Foundations for World Order' in H. Morgenthau and K. Thompson (eds.), *Principles and Problems of International Politics* (Knopf, 1950), p. 143. (Emphasis added.)
47 'Reforming World Order: Zones of Consciousness and Domains of Action' in Beres and Targ, *Alternative World Futures*, p. 198.
48 *The Future of Mankind*, English translation (University of Chicago Press, 1958), p. 14.
49 *Ibid.* p. 327.
50 R. Niebuhr, 'The Myth of World Government', *The Nation* (March 16, 1949); reproduced in Morgenthau and Thompson, *International Politics*, p. 137.
51 For an example of a less than optimistic appraisal, see A. J. Miller, 'Doomsday Politics: Prospects for International Co-operation', *International Journal*, 28, no. 1 (1972), 122–33.
52 W. Wagar, *Building the City of Man* (Freeman and Co., 1971), p. 29.
53 *Civilization in Crisis*, p. 185.
54 Preface in W. Wagar (ed.), *History and the Idea of Mankind* (University of New Mexico Press, 1971), p. vii.
55 *Endangered Planet*, p. 101.
56 Falk, 'Reforming World Order', p. 198.
57 A. Rapoport, *Strategy and Conscience* (Harper and Row, 1964), pp. 25–30.
58 *Ibid.* p. 25.
59 *Ibid.* p. 30.
60 *Ibid.*
61 See Mendlovitz's general introduction to the WOMP series, 'Preferred Worlds for the 1990's'.
62 Quoted in J. A. R. Marriott, *Commonwealth or Anarchy? A Survey of Projects of Peace* (Columbia University Press, 1939), p. 76.
63 Hinsley, *Power and Pursuit of Peace*, p. 1.
64 Quoted in Forsyth *et al.*, *International Relations*, p. 183.
65 Bull, *Anarchical Society*, p. 262.
66 L. P. Shields and M. C. Ott, 'The Environmental Crisis: International and Supranational Approaches', *International Relations*, 4, no. 6 (November 1974), 645–6.
67 *Ibid.* p. 647.
68 'To Prevent a World Wasteland: A Proposal', *Foreign Affairs*, no. 3 (April 1970), 413.
69 A. Rapoport, *Conflict in Man-Made Environment* (Penguin, 1974), p. 162.
70 Mannheim, *Ideology and Utopia*, pp. 190–205.
71 *Ibid.* p. 201.
72 *The Future of Mankind*, p. 324.

3 ROUSSEAU AND THE TRADITION OF DESPAIR

1 B. Porter, 'Patterns of Thought and Practice: Martin Wight's International Theory,' in M. Donelan (ed.), *The Reason of States* (Allen and Unwin, 1978), p. 71.
2 Evans, 'Some Problems', p. 720.
3 Waltz, 'International Relations', in Greenstein and Polsby, *International Politics*, p. 35.
4 F. Parkinson, *The Philosophy of International Relations*, Sage Library of Social Research, 52 (Sage Publications, 1977), p. 158.
5 'The Theory of International Politics 1919–1969' in Porter, *Aberystwyth Papers*, p. 36.
6 Quoted in Thompson, *Political Realism*, p. 31.
7 *The Nation-State and the Crisis of World Politics* (D. McKay, 1976), p. 74.
8 *Ibid.* pp. 72–3.
9 E. L. Morse, *Modernization and the Transformation of International Relations* (Free Press, 1976), p. 37.
10 F. Ajami, 'The Global Logic of the Neoconservatives', *World Politics* (April 1978), 463.
11 R. Niebuhr, *The Structure of Nations and Empires* (Scribner's, 1959), pp. 292–3.
12 *Twenty Years' Crisis*, pp. 87–8.
13 'World Government', p. 289.
14 R. W. Fox, 'Reinhold Niebuhr and the Emergence of the Liberal Realist Faith, 1930–1945', *The Review of Politics*, 38, no. 2 (April 1976), 247.
15 Thompson, *Political Realism*, p. 160.
16 R. Jervis, 'Co-operation under the Security Dilemma', *World Politics*, (January 1978), 167.
17 Meinecke, *Machiavellism*, p. 15.
18 Forsyth *et al.*, *International Relations*, p. 167. All quotations from Rousseau are taken from the selection of his writings reproduced in this book.
19 *Ibid.* p. 132.
20 'Knowledge, the State and the State of Nature' in Donelan, *Reason of States*, p. 119.
21 Forsyth *et al.*, *International Relations*, p. 132.
22 *Ibid.* p. 156.
23 *Ibid.*
24 *International Relations*, p. 150.
25 *Ibid.*
26 'Rousseau on War and Peace', p. 321.
27 Quoted in K. Waltz, *Man, the State and War* (Columbia, 1954), p. 181.
28 Forsyth *et al.*, *International Relations*, p. 170.
29 *Ibid.* p. 175.

30   *Ibid.* p. 147.
31   *Ibid.* p. 131.
32   *Ibid.*
33   Hoffmann, 'Rousseau on War and Peace', p. 317.
34   H. J. Morgenthau, *Politics Amongst Nations*, 5th ed. (Knopf, 1973), p. 4.
35   *Ibid.* p. 6.
36   Niebuhr, *Nations and Empires*, p. 292.
37   *A World Restored* (Grosset and Dunlop, 1964), p. 317.
38   Quoted in R. Falk, 'What's wrong with Henry Kissinger's Foreign Policy?', *Alternatives* (March 1975), 88.
39   *A World Restored*, p. 2.
40   K. Thompson, 'Moral Reasoning in American Thought on War and Peace', *Review of Politics* (July 1977), 389.
41   *Nuclear Weapons and Foreign Policy* (Harper, 1957), p. 202.
42   'Moral Reasoning', p. 388.
43   Niebuhr, *Nations and Empires*, pp. 289–90.
44   Carr, *Twenty Years' Crisis*, p. 93.
45   G. Evans, 'E. H. Carr and International Relations', *British Journal of International Studies*, 1 (1975), 89.
46   In Thompson, 'Moral Reasoning', p. 392.
47   *Ibid.* p. 393.
48   Morgenthau, *Politics Amongst Nations*, p. 10.
49   See his 'Idealism and Realism: Beyond the Great Debate', *British Journal of International Studies*, 3 (1977).
50   Meinecke, *Machiavellism*, pp. 15–16.
51   *A World Restored*, p. 316.
52   *American Foreign Policy* (Norton, 1969), p. 46.
53   Thompson, *Political Realism*, ch. 4.
54   Quoted by Thompson in 'Moral Reasoning', p. 390.
55   *Politics Amongst Nations*, p. 5.
56   Thompson, *Political Realism*, p. 3.
57   Burns, *Of Powers*, p. 3.
58   J. W. Burton, *World Society* (C.U.P., 1972), p. 90.
59   *The Story of Utopias* (Viking Edition, 1962), pp. 8–9.

4   FROM BALANCE TO CONCERT: 1815–1854

1   See in particular C. Bell, *The Conventions of Crisis: A Study in Diplomatic Management* (O.U.P., 1971).
2   I. C. Nichols, *The European Pentarchy and the Congress of Verona, 1822* (Nijhoff, 1971), p. 326.
3   F. Northedge and M. Grieve, *A Hundred Years of International Relations* (Duckworth, 1971), p. 200.
4   *Ibid.* pp. 278–9.
5   R. B. Elrod, 'The Concert of Europe: A Fresh Look at an International System', *World Politics* (January 1976), 167.

6 R. Albrecht-Carrié, *The Concert of Europe 1815–1914* (Harper, 1968); p. 5.
7 'Concert of Europe', p. 163.
8 P. W. Schroeder, *Austria, Great Britain and the Crimean War: The Destruction of the European Concert* (Cornell, 1972), p. 409.
9 W. N. Medlicott, *Bismarck, Gladstone and the Concert of Europe* (Athlone Press, 1956), p. 18.
10 C. Holbraad, 'Condominium and Concert' in Holbraad (ed.), *Super Powers and World Order* (Australian National University, 1971), p. 13. See also C. Holbraad, *The Concert of Europe* (Longman, 1970).
11 *Swords into Plowshares.*
12 *Ibid.* p. 24.
13 The whole point about Bell's 'Conventions of Crisis' is that they circumvent, or are a substitute for, the organisational machinery of the United Nations.
14 *Austria, Britain, Crimean War*, p. 404. (Emphasis added.)
15 'Concert of Europe', p. 161.
16 M. Wright (ed.), *The Theory and Practice of the Balance of Power* (Dent, 1975), pp. xiv–xv.
17 *Ibid.* p. xviii.
18 E. V. Gulick, *Europe's Classical Balance of Power* (Norton Edition, 1967).
19 *Ibid.* p. 159.
20 *Ibid.* pp. 305–6.
21 Hinsley, *Power and Pursuit of Peace*, p. 225.
22 *Bismarck, Gladstone, Concert of Europe*, p. 18.
23 F. S. Northedge, *The International Political System* (Faber and Faber, 1976), p. 84.
24 'Concert of Europe', p. 160.
25 G. Goodwin, 'International Institutions and International Order' in James, *International Order*, p. 163.
26 Hinsley, *Power and Pursuit of Peace*, p. 226.
27 Holbraad, 'Condominium and Concert', p. 15.
28 'Concert of Europe', pp. 172–3.
29 *Austria, Britain, Crimean War*, p. 407.
30 *Concert of Europe*, pp. 15–16. (Emphases added.)
31 *Bismarck, Gladstone, Concert of Europe*, p. 18.
32 *Concert of Europe*, p. 17.
33 *Ibid.* p. 19.

5 BALANCE WITHOUT CONCERT: 1856–1914

1 Some analysts, for instance, argue that there was a major change during the 1870s alone. See B. Healy and A. Stein, 'The Balance of Power in International History', *Journal of Conflict Resolution*, 17, no. 3 (September 1973).
2 J. Joll, *Europe Since 1870* (Weidenfeld and Nicolson, 1973), ch. 1.

3 Hinsley, *Power and Pursuit of Peace*, p. 249.
4 *Ibid.* p. 254.
5 *The Ascendancy of Europe* (Longman, 1972), pp. 54–5.
6 *The Struggle for Mastery in Europe* (O.U.P., 1954), p. 82.
7 G. Barraclough, *An Introduction to Contemporary History* (Penguin, 1964), pp. 98–9.
8 F. Fischer, *Germany's Aims in the First World War* (Norton, 1967).
9 Northedge and Grieve, *International Relations*, p. 81.
10 *Struggle for Mastery*, p. 336.

6 CONCERT WITHOUT BALANCE: 1918–1939

1 A. J. Mayer, *Political Origins of the New Diplomacy* (Yale University Press, 1959).
2 R. Albrecht-Carrié, *The Unity of Europe* (Secker and Warburg, 1966), p. 199.
3 A. Zimmern, *The League of Nations and the Rule of Law* (Macmillan, 1936), p. 137.
4 Schwarzenberger, *Power Politics*, p. 273.
5 From an extract in A. Lijphart (ed.), *World Politics*, 2nd ed. (Allyn and Bacon, 1971), p. 290.
6 Zimmern, *League of Nations*, p. 78.
7 *Ibid.* p. 110.
8 Claude, *Swords Into Plowshares*, p. 38.
9 *Ibid.* p. 44.
10 *Twenty Years' Crisis*.
11 *Ibid.* p. 87.
12 *Ibid.*
13 *Politics and Diplomacy of Peacemaking* (Weidenfeld and Nicolson, 1968).
14 Quoted *ibid.* p. 12.
15 The tension between 'universalist' and 'exclusivist' conceptions of the League's membership is described in G. Schwarzenberger, *The League of Nations and World Order* (Constable, 1936).

7 FROM CONCERT TO BALANCE: 1945–1980

1 M. Wight, 'The Balance of Power and International Order' in James, *International Order*, p. 113.
2 *Ibid.* p. 112.
3 *A World Restored*, p. 1.
4 *Anarchical Society*, p. 207.
5 *Ibid.*
6 *Anarchical Society*, p. 212.
7 A. Buchan, *Power and Equilibrium in the 1970's* (Praeger, 1973), p. 16.
8 See e.g. A. Burns, 'From Balance to Deterrence', *World Politics*, 9 (1957); G. Snyder, 'The Balance of Power and the Balance of

Terror', in Lijphart, *World Politics*; J. H. Herz, 'Balance Systems and Balance Politics in a Nuclear and Bipolar Age' in P. Toma and A. Gyorgy (eds.), *Basic Issues in International Relations* (Allyn and Bacon, 1967).

9 M. Wight, 'The Balance of Power' in Butterfield and Wight, *Diplomatic Investigations*, p. 167.

10 V. P. Lukin, 'American–Chinese Relations: Concept and Reality', *U.S.A.–Economics, Politics, Ideology*, No 2 (February 1973).

11 Moscow Radio, 1 August 1971.

12 Lukin, *ibid*. For an elaboration of this argument, see the present author's 'Sino-American Relations in Soviet Perspective', *Orbis* (summer 1973).

13 Herz, *Nation-State*, p. 59.

14 Keohane and Nye, *Power and Interdependence*, p. 8.

15 J. Lewis, 'Oil, other Scarcities and the poor countries', *World Politics* (October 1974), 69.

16 E.g. J. Nye, 'Collective Economic Security', *International Affairs* (October 1974).

17 Lewis, 'Oil and poor countries', p. 64.

18 Keohane and Nye, *Power and Interdependence*, p. 35.

19 'The Growth of International Institutions' in Porter, *Aberystwyth Papers*, p. 286.

20 Inis Claude, *Power and International Relations* (Random House, 1962), p. 160.

21 Goodwin, 'International Institutions' in James, *International Order*, p. 160.

22 *Ibid.* p. 183.

23 A. LeRoy Bennett, *International Organizations* (Prentice-Hall, 1977), p. 389.

24 'Balance of Power', in James, *International Order*, p. 111.

25 Bennett, *International Organizations*, p. 132.

26 T. C. Schelling, *Arms and Influence* (Yale, 1966), p. 3.

27 R. Osgood and R. Tucker, *Force, Order and Justice* (Johns Hopkins, 1967), p. 26.

28 *Ibid.* p. 15.

29 *Ibid.* p. 225.

30 P. Keal, 'Spheres of Influence and International Order' (Ph.D. thesis, Department of International Relations, Australian National University).

31 E. Kaufman, *The Superpowers and their Spheres of Influence* (Croom Helm, 1976), p. 10.

32 *Anarchical Society*, p. 206.

33 *Ibid.* p. 224.

34 *The Superpowers*, p. 23.

35 P. Williams, *Crisis Management* (Martin Robertson, 1976), p. 28.

36 *Conventions of Crisis*.

37 *Ibid.* p. 75.

38   *The Diplomacy of Detente* (St Martin's Press, 1977), p. vii.
39   *Ibid.* p. 5.
40   *Ibid.*
41   *Detente*, p. 25.
42   *Anarchical Society*, pp. 226–7.
43   Morse, *Modernization*, p. 44.
44   *Ibid.* p. 45.

CONCLUSION: FULL CIRCLE?

1   Pp. 3–4.
2   Paul Taylor, 'International Relations Theory, the Idea of Progress and the Role of the International Civil Servant', *Political Studies*, 20, no. 3 (1972), 268.
3   'An American Social Science: International Relations', *Daedalus* (Summer 1977), 57.
4   A. Bozeman, *Politics and Culture in International History* (Princeton, 1960).
5   'On the Performance of the International Polity', *British Journal of International Studies*, 4 (1978), 191.
6   'The World Order Models Project and its Critics: A Reply', *International Organization* (spring 1978), 542.
7   *Politics and Culture*, p. 520.
8   J. Weltman, 'On the Obsolescence of War: An Essay in Policy and Theory', *International Studies Quarterly* (December 1974), 405.
9   F. A. M. Alting von Geusau, *European Perspectives on World Order* (Sijthoff, 1975), p. 301.
10   N. Mandelbaum, 'International Stability and Nuclear Order: the first Nuclear Regime', in D. Gompert, M. Mandelbaum, R. L. Garwin and J. H. Barton, *Nuclear Weapons and World Politics* (McGraw-Hill, 1977).
11   There is an extensive body of literature on this question. For recent contributions, see e.g. G. Snyder and P. Diesing, *Conflict Among Nations* (Princeton, 1977), ch. 6; also C. Ostrom and J. Aldrich, 'The Relationship between Size and Stability in the Major Power International System', *American Journal of Political Science*, 22, no. 4 (November 1978).
12   E. Luard, *Types of International Society* (Free Press, 1976), p. 303.
13   'Performance', p. 197.
14   *Whig Interpretation*, p. 11.
15   R. J. Vincent, 'Western Conceptions of a Universal Moral Order', *British Journal of International Studies*, 4 (April 1978), 37.
16   'Performance', p. 199.
17   P. Savigear, 'European Political Philosophy and International Relations' in T. Taylor (ed.), *Approaches and Theory in International Relations* (Longman, 1978), p. 35. The same point has been made by

M. Wight. See his 'Why is there no International Theory?' in Butterfield and Wight, *Diplomatic Investigations*.

18 Quoted in S. Pollard, *The Idea of Progress* (Penguin, 1971), p. 167.
19 H. Foley (ed.), *Woodrow Wilson's Case for the League of Nations* (Kennikat, 1967), p. 64.
20 Taylor, 'International Relations Theory', p. 267.
21 *Ibid.*
22 See e.g. R. Rothstein, *The Weak in the World of the Strong* (Columbia, 1977).
23 For one discussion of this relationship, see J. Galtung, 'The New Economic Order in World Politics' in A. W. Singham (ed.), *The Nonaligned Movement in World Politics* (Lawrence Hill, 1977).
24 G. Liska, *Quest for Equilibrium* (Johns Hopkins, 1977), p. ix.
25 *Power and Equilibrium*, p. 111.

Index